Sex Work and the City

Inter-America Series
Duncan Earle, Howard Campbell, and John Peterson, editors
In the new "Inter-American" epoch to come, our borderland zones may expand well past the confines of geopolitical lines. Social knowledge of these dynamic interfaces offers rich insights into the pressing and complex issues that affect both the borderlands and beyond. The Inter-America Series comprises a wide interdisciplinary range of cutting-edge books that explicitly or implicitly enlist border issues to discuss larger concepts, perspectives, and theories from the "borderland" vantage and will be appropriate for the classroom, the library, and the wider reading public.

Sex Work and the City

The Social Geography of Health
and Safety in Tijuana, Mexico

YASMINA KATSULIS

University of Texas Press ⟪⟫ *Austin*

Requests for permission to reproduce material from this work should be sent to:
    Permissions
    University of Texas Press
    P.O. Box 7819
    Austin, TX 78713-7819
    www.utexas.edu/utpress/about/bpermission.html

♾ The paper used in this book meets the minimum requirements of
ANSI/NISO Z39.48-1992 (R1997) (Permanence of Paper).

Library of Congress Cataloging-in-Publication Data
Katsulis, Yasmina, 1972–
    Sex work and the city : the social geography of health and safety in
Tijuana, Mexico / Yasmina Katsulis. — 1st ed.
        p.   cm. — Inter-America Series, Duncan Earle, Howard Campbell,
and John Peterson series editors
    Includes bibliographical references and index.
    ISBN 978-0-292-71886-9 (cloth : alk. paper)
    1. Prostitution—Mexico—Tijuana.   2. Prostitutes—Mexico—Tijuana.
I. Title.   II. Series.
    HQ151.T54K37   2008
    306.740972′23—dc22
                                                          2008012815

For Jeff, who supports me in all things that matter.

Contents

Preface

I grew up in California near a town called Nevada City. Established in 1849, Nevada City was a prosperous gold mining town, one of many in California. As a young girl, I visited its historic buildings and Victorian houses and marveled at the luxurious hand-carved stairways and dark red carpets of its stagecoach hotel. Just a few doors from the hotel stood a grand three-story building now used as a restaurant. It was filled with fine antique furniture, velvet-papered walls, and finely wrought mirrored sconces. A long oak bar and a player piano stood prominently in the center of its large first floor. When a friend of the family took over the business, I gained access to the upper floors, which had sat unused and empty for many decades. It was a tenement house of sorts, and, as a young girl is wont to do, I wandered about dreamily, looking for bits of evidence of lives left behind.

Only later was I told that it was a "whorehouse," long since abandoned by the history of the town. I could only imagine what its residents' lives had been like. Who were they, the women who had lived and worked here? why had they come to this frontier town so far from the bustling Eastern seaboard? had they found happiness here or misery? what became of them? Little did I know then that I would continue to ask similar questions about "working women" of the Californias. Having traveled all the way to the East Coast to pursue my doctorate, I returned to the West—to Tijuana, Mexico, a border town containing many of the same human elements left behind by the history of Nevada City, only on a *much* larger scale. This book is a product of those questions I asked as a girl in Nevada City and answered so many years later in Tijuana, a frontier town that is now the world's most frequently visited border city.

In thinking about a field project, I initially wrote a number of grant applications to study Mexican housewives, normative sexuality, and risk for HIV/

AIDS. Having completed a project in college on normative sexual practices among Catholic college students, I was eager to explore the topic further by studying how housewives manage sexual risk within relationships that, while understood on an ideological level to be risk-free, are the primary route of infection for women across the world. I soon realized that because of the paucity of epidemiological evidence needed to persuade funding organizations that this was a topic worthy of study, each application was rejected (the funding climate surrounding the study of normative sexuality has changed somewhat since I submitted those first applications in 1998). Nothing if not practical, and needing to obtain funding to support my dissertation research, I eventually modified my proposals. Although I ended up receiving a grant to study the sex workers upon which this book is based, and although I am confident that the project led to useful and interesting findings, I must begin with this small caveat. My experience in trying to get funding for this project reflects the general funding climate that surrounds public health research on HIV/AIDS and the continued reinforcement of prostitute sexuality as deviant, dangerous, and polluting. Funding organizations continue to be attracted to ideas about sexual deviance and the dangers it appears to represent. Ironically, the commodification of sexuality, particularly women's sexuality, is *anything but* deviant, although its more obvious forms continue to be subject to public scrutiny and social control.

While I will always be grateful for the financial support I received, it's very important to me that my readers understand how we, as social scientists, become socialized to reproduce and reinforce the surveillance of so-called deviant sexualities, even when we begin with a very different agenda. Having decided to become at least somewhat compliant does not mean I failed to approach this study through a critical framework. First, although sexual health research in the era of HIV/AIDS tends to concentrate on female prostitution or male homosexuality or both, I sought to disrupt these stereotypes by including male, transgender, and female sex workers in my study and to focus on the gendered dimensions of sexual behavior within the industry. Work-related sexual behavior is also not conflated with assumptions of sexual orientation, and data on partnering practices were collected with a greater level of specificity than one might find in other studies. In addition, although funding was available through the National Security Administration for the study of Mexican sexualities as a national security issue for the United States, I instead concentrated on seeking basic science funding through the National Science Foundation Americas Program. Also, in setting up this study I used every tool I knew of to avoid reinforcing the common stereotype of prostitutes as dangerous vectors of disease in need of control from above. I approached this topic with the idea that while there was bound to be a high level of diversity among sex workers, it was likely that, in comparison with their peers who were not sex workers, sex workers were more likely to be aware of sexual risks and more likely to take precautions to minimize them, at least when they were able to. I believe this is so for a number of reasons: sex workers have greater experience in the realm of sexual activity; they are likely to have more skill in negotiating sexual activities with their partners and controlling the sexual transaction; and finally, they are likely to more correctly identify and be aware of treatment options for sexually transmitted infections, including HIV/AIDS, and to understand and be actively engaged in protecting their reproductive health. Indeed, we now know that in the United States, for example, non-drug-using female sex workers consistently require their customers to use condoms in their commercial transactions, but not in their nonwork sexual relationships with boyfriends or husbands and are therefore more likely to become infected with a sexually transmitted infection through normative relationships than through sexual relations at work. The negotiation of occupational health risks does, however, take place within a multilayered context of intersecting social positions. Those who have the most difficult time negotiating these risks are women who are largely poor, who are often from a rural or indigenous background, and who often lack the documentation or are not of legal age to work legally. Transgender and youth sex workers also have a difficult time because of their place in the general social hierarchy. Drug-addicted sex workers, who may use sex work as a way to support their addiction, have a very difficult time negotiating safer sex at work because of the potential loss of income. On the other hand, those at the top of the sex work hierarchy as well as those involved in the sex workers' union have an easier time protecting both their financial interests and their physical safety at work. Thus social location within the hierarchy has a direct impact on workplace health and safety, making considerations such as social mobility, legal issues, and policy issues integral to understanding and minimizing sex workers' risk.

When some members of the local sex workers' union, tired of public health scrutiny and interference, remained skeptical and resentful of my project, I became frustrated, but I understood. As a researcher studying sex workers' health, particularly sexual health issues, I was perceived as part of the much larger picture of social control and body regulation that city officials, police, policymakers, and scientists enact through interventions that target prostitutes as reservoirs of infectious disease. However, I was convinced I could use this research as an opportunity to broaden the debate by moving beyond individual risk behavior in the sexual domain to incorporate the social determinants of occupational health and specifically the complex relationships among social hierarchy, working conditions, and occupational risk. This was also an opportunity, as I saw it, to broaden the way in which the health of sex workers is perceived, in that it should encompass more than genital health and include those aspects of health and safety seen as a significant priority among workers themselves, namely, workplace violence, mental health, drug use and addiction, social stigma, and human rights abuses by police.

Note: All photos are by the author. All *gender-based* tables refer to survey data collected from female (N=140), male (N=42), and transgender (N=16) sex workers involved in this study. All *legal status* tables refer to survey data collected from female sex workers only and are categorized as either Registered Female Sex Workers (RFSW) (N=33) or Unregistered Female Sex Workers (UFSW) (N=107).

Acknowledgments

Thank you, mom and dad, for encouraging my love of learning from the beginning and for your unwavering support of my dreams over the years. You made it possible for me to think as big as I wanted. Mary Ann and Hutch—thank you for taking such pride in my accomplishments, for supporting me as I went to school, and for always treating me like your own. Thank you, Marcus, E, Tony, Brian, Charlotte, Shannon, and Christine—thank you for your friendship and encouragement and for making me remember I am more than my work. Thank you, John L., for your friendship in the field and for helping me through what would have been a much more difficult time without you. Linda-Anne, your friendship and mentorship have been crucial, but, more than that, you have accepted me for who I am, and for that I will always be grateful. A big thank you to my new mentors at the Women and Gender Studies Program at Arizona State University—Rose Weitz, Mary Logan Rothschild, Mary Margaret Fonow, Lisa M. Anderson, Maria Luz Cruz-Torres, Ann Koblitz, Karen J. Leong, Alesha Durfee, Jill A. Fisher, and Georganne Scheiner Gillis, your unwavering support and general enthusiasm mean the world to me.

To my husband, Jeff, there comes a point when words can't capture the gratitude and love someone has for another person. We have been in it together from the beginning, and we are stronger than ever. You made it possible for me to follow my passion, even when it made things difficult. You are an inspiration to me—in the contributions you provide through your work, in your willingness and ability to take on any task, and in your talent for understanding, compassion, and generosity. You are everything to me.

This book began as a doctoral dissertation for Yale University under the direction of Linda-Anne Rebhun, Enrique Mayer, Nora Groce, and Kim Blankenship. Thank you so much for your guidance and encouragement. I am indebted to you for your insights on my early draft materials as well as your professional guidance and mentorship. I would also like to thank my field collaborators, Drs. Roberto Ham-Chande and Gudelia Rangel of the Department of Population Studies at El Colegio de la Frontera Norte (COLEF), Dra. Remedios Lozada of ISESALUD (Tijuana), Dr. Pedro Lopez of Servicios Médicos Municipales, Tijuana (SMM), and the director and staff at SMM for their assistance in supplying background materials for this project. Thank you for your time, advice, and institutional support.

This book would not have been possible without generous financial support from the National Science Foundation America's Program, the Yale Center for International Area Studies, the Yale Graduate School of Arts and Sciences, the National Institute of Mental Health, and the Yale Center for Interdisciplinary Research on AIDS. Preliminary research and language preparation were supported by the Andrew Mellon Foundation and the U.S. Department of Education Foreign Language and Area Studies Program. I am profoundly grateful to the scientists at the Yale Center for Interdisciplinary Research on AIDS for offering me their scientific expertise as well as the time necessary to complete my manuscript. For their comments on various portions of this manuscript, I am particularly indebted to Kim Blankenship, Merrill Singer, and Jeannette Ickovics. For their general encouragement and support, I also wish to thank Tina Hopey, Leif Mitchell, Robert Heimer, Kaveh Khoshnood, Robert Dubrow, David Paltiel, Robert Levine, Kathleen Sikkema, and Michael Merson. Any errors are my own.

Finally, this project would not have been possible without help from the following individuals at the University of Texas. Thank you for your patience, guidance, and careful proofreading of my manuscript: Theresa May, editor-in-chief, Samantha Allison, manuscript editor, the copyeditor Larry Kenney, and Howard Campbell.

Sex Work and the City

Introduction

Health policy formation and implementation unfold in a world of competitive social interests, opposed class agendas, unequal genders, and overt and covert power conflicts. Health policy may produce structural violence, defined as the set of large-scale social forces, such as racism, sexism, political violence, poverty, and other social inequalities, which are rooted in historical and economic processes. As a result, health-related policies, which have the ostensive goal of improving and protecting the health of the general public or sectors thereof, may, in their service of other masters, harm rather than enhance public health.
MERRILL SINGER AND ARACHU CASTRO, 2004

Background

This book is based on eighteen months of intensive anthropological field research conducted in Tijuana, Mexico (2000–2001). My primary goals were, first, to document the experiences of a diverse range of sex workers who live and work on the U.S.-Mexican border, and, second, to understand the impact of one's location in the social hierarchy on occupational health and safety. Although municipal laws, policies, and practices are shaped by existing social relations outside of the industry, they have a profound effect on social hierarchy within the sex industry itself. They may shift existing power relations, providing new arenas in which power can be claimed or negotiated. Alternatively, they may reinforce existing disparities and further disenfranchise those already marginalized by their position in society. An understanding of these complex relationships is therefore essential in developing effective programs and policies that positively impact sex workers' health and safety.

A variety of disciplines, from feminist social ecology to spatial epidemiology, have adopted, created, and transformed the concept of social geography in an effort to understand a multiplicity of social locations within the increasingly complex postmodern landscape. Feminist geography, for example, emphasizes the centrality of the body as a site of material, symbolic, and political struggle.[1] It is a springboard for understanding everything from the gendered impact of economic development in industrializing countries to the polemics of sexual citizenship and gay marriage in the United States. Local struggles about prostitution law and policy form part of a larger story in which we tell ourselves which bodies need to be regulated and policed and which are safe to ignore. The bodies of prostitutes, prisoners, and immigrants, for example, tend to be seen as sources of danger and treated accordingly, whereas the bodies of "good citizens," however that locution is defined, tend to be viewed as embodiments of the sacred.

As the title of this book suggests, the concept of social geography and the mapping of health disparities and social difference are central to my approach in this book. The mapping of this social geography, if thought of in visual terms, would represent a series of intersecting continuums of power, identity, and difference upon which sex workers with a variety of background characteristics are located. Their locations, however, are not necessarily determined by their past so much as they are shaped and influenced by it. They are also shaped by the ways in which these social actors choose to navigate this complex social environment. These choices should be understood as rational (as opposed to a free choice), according to the distinction made by sex worker activists who acknowledge varying levels of opportunity, agency, and coercion constraining the decision-making ability and autonomy of the social actors involved. In this way, one's social location as a sex worker is incredibly significant in shaping not only the occupational risks one is exposed to, but also one's ability to negotiate or avoid those risks.

My definition of occupational health and safety is intentionally broad, encompassing quality of life issues, mental health, substance use and addiction, social stigma, and violence as well as the more familiar sexual health issues linked to the sex industry. In order to understand the effect of legalization on sex workers' occupational health, I approached this research with the following strategies in mind: (1) to compare occupational risk exposure and health outcomes between sex workers who work legally and those who work illegally; (2) to identify the impact of legal status on working conditions as well as the ability to negotiate improved working conditions; (3) to identify barriers to working legally; and (4) to generate ideas for structural interventions to improve health and safety. This approach raised interesting methodological challenges in terms of gaining access to what is essentially a bifurcated system with two sectors coexisting in the same geographical area—one formal, well organized, and legal, the other informal, individualistic, and criminalized.

Because sex work in Tijuana has a quasi-legal status (that is, it is neither explicitly legal nor illegal in law), the response to it has been mixed and varied over time. Grounded in a politics of difference that singles out some groups and geographical areas and ignores others, law enforcement and health inspectors have helped to create a social hierarchy of sex work that mirrors everyday relations of power intersected by gendered, classed, and racialized differences. While the harm reduction approach popularized by public health advocates emphasizes legal regulation, licensing, registration, and mandatory health screening, barriers to registration and licensing effectively limit the benefits of legal status to those at the top of the social hierarchy and further marginalize those at the bottom. Crackdowns by law enforcement fine, shut down, and imprison those who work illegally, thereby increasing their vulnerabilities, exacerbating their occupational risks, and limiting their ability to respond to these risks.

Sex workers (rather than their customers) have been conventionally portrayed as a bridge between low- and high-risk groups, a "disease vector" that in most countries has been controlled through various legal and public health mechanisms for hundred of years. Research on sex workers' health is generally conceived of in very narrow terms. Sex workers tend to be viewed not in terms of their human complexity, but as prostitutes first and foremost, while other aspects of their lives that may influence their approach to sex work, their experiences while at work, their motivations to work, their family roles and responsibilities, and so on are ignored. When their personal histories are documented, it is often to present a picture of family dysfunction or sexual abuse or both, an inability to function in other forms of work, vulnerability to being manipulated by a pimp, and an inability to form affective attachments. Their lives are individuated and pathologized, while the political and economic factors that ensure an increasing supply of sex workers to serve an increasing demand for their services are rendered invisible. Often the nature of their work, because it includes sex, has been sexualized to the point that other aspects of the workplace are overlooked, discouraging a more systematic analysis of organizational dynamics, labor rights issues, and workplace health and safety. Thus nearly all public health research on sex work tends to focus on sexually transmitted infections (sTIs) and, more recently, on HIV/AIDS, while other health and safety issues are disregarded.

In many countries, legalization of commercial sex work activities has been supported in order to reduce infectious disease among sex workers, their customers, and their customers' partners. Legalization has been conceived as a harm reduction measure meant to improve the health outcomes of sex workers by enforcing mandatory screening and treatment of STIs, including HIV/AIDS, presumably reducing their prevalence among sex workers. The impact of legalization on working conditions and other aspects of workplace health and safety, whether positive or negative, is unknown. Additionally, although the prevalence of STIs and HIV/AIDS among sex workers varies widely from country to country—it is less than 1 percent in some areas but as high as 90 percent in others—the effect of harm reduction through legalization has not been studied systematically. Outside of STI treatment and screening, little attention is paid to the effect of legal status on working conditions, conditions which are relevant not only to STI prevention and risk avoidance, but also to the many competing health and safety issues faced by workers. There is seldom any acknowledgment of those who continue to work illegally, no real engagement with the complexities of, and barriers to, legal status, and little attention to the disparate health outcomes between those who work illegally and those who work legally. Last, there is a need to develop an understanding of occupational health issues among migrant sex workers and those who serve migrant workers. The migration issue points toward the importance of political economy and social change, but additionally is at the center of debates about human trafficking, identity politics, and struggles over sexual citizenship. The volition of migrant sex workers, for example, is often denied or ignored in debates about human trafficking, whereas the rights of migrant sex workers to register and work legally are often limited because of citizenship and documentation restrictions. Thus our understanding of the special circumstances of migrant labor within the sex industry and of the relationship between migration status and occupational health and safety desperately needs to be developed through rigorous scientific research.

I found Tijuana, Mexico, to be the ideal location for this study. It is a city located on the busiest migration corridor in the western hemisphere, and the reputation of its legalized sex industry is fairly well known. When I arrived in Tijuana to begin my research, I was assaulted from every direction by commercialized sexual exchange. Recruitment posters, street workers, strip clubs, neighborhood gossip, planned expeditions—much of my new social world revolved around the most visible form of cross-border sexual relations, Tijuana's commercial sex industry. According to the city clinic that serves legal sex workers in Tijuana, approximately one thousand sex workers are currently working legally in Tijuana, with about three hundred newly legal workers replacing those who leave the industry each year. The number of full-time sex workers who work illegally is unknown. Based on my empirical observations of those whom I saw coming into the clinic (legal sex workers) and those obviously working but not participating in clinic services (and therefore illegal), I estimate that the number of those working illegally is much, much higher than those who work legally. In many parts of the city one can observe a thriving local sex trade, and these areas are not targeted by the health inspectors, who enforce mandatory registration and screening. In addition, certainly a large number work on a part-time basis to make ends meet. In fact, the majority of the sex workers discussed in this book engaged in sex work part-time before officially registering with the clinic. Those who are new to the city often work full-time without registering, until health inspectors and police make this option less appealing. After being threatened, fined, or jailed, some come to the clinic to register only to be told that because of their age or documentation status they aren't eligible to work legally. As a result, many continue to work illegally regardless of the consequences and simply do their best to work in areas where they are less likely to be caught or hassled by inspectors or police. Those who work illegally are not only greater in number, but also the most vulnerable to extortion, manipulation, and violence, and they have little legal recourse owing to their fear of prosecution.

Although there is no estimate of the total population of sex workers in Mexico, it has been increasingly recognized that Mexico is a favored destination for U.S. and European sex tourists (Hughes 1999), as evidenced by the fact that most homeless girls accessing shelter services have engaged in sex work before entering the shelter system (Harris 1997). Reflecting the unequal social standing of the United States and its neighbor to the south, the huge commercial sex industry in Tijuana came into existence primarily to serve the sexual needs, desires, and fantasies of American men; however, the enormous flow of Mexican and Central American male migrants traveling through the city has ensured a growing demand for the industry. Although U.S. tourists are easy to spot in the Zona Norte, the majority of customers seen in the red light areas and elsewhere are Latino migrants, not tourists. This migratory flow, as I illustrate in chapter 1, is closely tied to the historical and contemporary relationship between the United States and Mexico. The supply of and demand for prostitution on the border will continue to expand if these larger demographic shifts remain unchanged.

The growth of a highly commercialized sex industry marked by national and international trade and migration is not unique to the U.S.-Mexico border. Although commercial sex work is a widespread and visible phenomenon, it has been difficult to estimate the extent of industry worldwide because of its illicit nature. Additionally, in many countries, estimates come from a variety of sources using different methods and definitions. That such reports are not always explicit about those methods or definitions makes it impossible to correlate comparative data between national sources. Statistical referents are necessarily partial and flawed.

The portrait painted by these disparate sources, however, remains bleak. It is estimated that two million girls between the ages of five and fifteen are introduced into the commercial sex market each year (UNIFEM 2003), a market which includes up to forty-six million women worldwide.[2] In Southeast Asia, the sex industry can account for up to 14 percent of gross domestic product (GDP), and remittances from sex workers to rural families sometimes exceed the entire budget of government-funded development programs (Lim 1998). Many of the six to eight hundred thousand persons who travel illegally across international borders each year are involved in the commercial sex trade (U.S. Department of State 2005). A recent report suggests that the number of commercial sex workers who migrate legally is estimated to exceed eight million (Health and Medicine Week 2004).

Measuring the extent of sex work is also complicated in that sex work exists on a continuum, with informal sexual exchange for a variety of resources, including food, shelter, and clothing, on the one hand, and commercialized sexual exchange on the other. Some activists in the area of sex work maintain that marriage itself is a form of sex work. Most of those who engage in informal kinds of sexual exchange don't identify themselves as sex workers, nor would they ever be arrested for their activities and counted in a national report. This book is about those who work on the commercialized end of the spectrum, for whom sex work has become the primary source of income.

Primary Findings

Although official discourse depicts sex work as a low-risk, harmless part of the entertainment industry in Tijuana, sex workers, like other workers, are at risk for a variety of health hazards related to their employment. The legalization model appears to benefit sex workers' health outcomes and reduce HIV risk among those who work legally, yet there are three problems with this model that may not be evident at first glance. First, there is little evidence of the impact of legalization on overall occupational risk among sex workers. Second, there is little official acknowledgment of those who continue to work illegally and hardly any research comparing health outcomes between these two groups. And third, given the likelihood that the subpopulation of those who work illegally is larger and that this group is likely to be the more vulnerable of the two, legalization as currently conceived is not enough.

The harm reduction approach offered by the city (legal regulations) has reduced occupational health risks for those women who are able to work legally.

However, official portrayals mask severe social inequalities and a decreasing quality of life among Mexican citizens and contrast strongly with the lived experience of occupational risks faced by those who work illegally. Sex work is one of few opportunities for socioeconomic advancement and family survival for poor women. Policy interventions must therefore consider the socioeconomic context of the sex industry, particularly as it is shaped by northward migration within Mexico, continuing gender disparities, and the lack of viable economic alternatives. Any intervention that focuses only on the individual behaviors of sex workers is unlikely to affect the larger social context which allows the sex industry to flourish.

These findings suggest that health interventions and policies related to sex work should acknowledge the impact of legal status and policing on sex workers, the social diversity and stratification of sex workers, and sex workers' health priorities, which may give risk for STIs a lower priority in reference to other occupational hazards, including violence, substance abuse, stress, and depression. Legal status and police practices mitigate or, in the case of illegal workers, increase occupational risks, including risk for extortion, violence, and rape perpetrated by police. The legal and regulatory framework found in Tijuana shapes the social organization and status hierarchy of the sex industry as well as the ability of sex workers not only to claim a more professional and legitimate social status, but also to transcend highly stratified class lines.

In presenting my case, I provide narrative and survey data from both legal and illegal workers, a detailed analysis of the current social organization of the sex industry in Tijuana, the relationship between the sex industry and the political economy of the border region, and the occupational risks that are navigated by sex workers at each level of this stratified hierarchy.

Sexual and economic exchanges take place along a continuum of formal/informal, short-term/long-term social relations, including marriage, casual partnering, and commercialized transactions. Those who are denied access to resources in the formal economy can trade sex for the money or protection provided by men, either in the form of formal sex work or, on a more informal basis, through boyfriends and husbands. Gender, age, and class configure these relations of power, just as they do the social hierarchy found within the industry. A culturally informed understanding of emotion, romance, money, and power is essential in connecting what appear to be highly diverse kinds of sexual relationships. Sex work transactions are not immune to these dynamics. The range of sexual exchanges within this sexual economy could all be considered types of sex "work"—making the study of commercial sexual exchange in isolation problematic.

However, in order to examine particular legal and policy issues more explicitly, I focus on the lived experiences of sex workers involved in formalized commercial sexual exchange. Literature regarding the effects of the legal status of sex work represents a growing debate among social and political scientists and activists. Although such discussions originated in the reformist periods of the United States and Europe, the increasing institutionalization of sex work in many countries makes these renewed debates very relevant in terms of public policy and international relations today.[3] While the debates regarding the ethics and efficacy of social control through regulation or criminalization are interesting theoretically, they often ignore the lived experience of the sex workers and customers who act within these legal systems.

The lived experience of sex workers often contradicts assumptions that are made on the basis of a generalized understanding of a criminal versus a legal, or regulated, sex work. First, in a system in which all sex work is criminalized, often only the most visible forms of outdoor, or street, sex work are policed, while indoor sex work through call services, escort agencies, the Internet, and massage parlors remains largely ignored. The existence of street sex work, which is the most visible evidence of an underground sex industry, continues unabated in most cities around the world. Although policing strategies can control the shape of the industry, the particular locations where it may occur, and the consequences of commercial sex transactions, they do not reduce the need for economic alternatives to sex work. The appearance of new solicitation sites following crackdowns is inevitable if there is no strong intervention program in place to offer alternatives. Policing strategies and the treatment of criminalized sex workers differ according to changing political demands—thus the experiences of, and the risks associated with, criminalization fluctuate according to the historical moment. Crackdowns are rarely sustained efforts; they are generally short-term events that give the appearance of solving the problem while only moving it further underground.

In a system in which sex work is regulated through legal means, as is the case in Tijuana, the impact of those regulations varies according to one's position within the formal and legal or informal and illegal sector. In a regulated system, legal age, documentation, and citizenship status largely determine whether one is allowed to work legally within that system. In addition, classed, gendered, and racialized physical attributes and conceptions of beauty form the structure of social stratification within this hierarchy and determine the kind of work venue that is available to any particular individual. Because the work venue plays such a strong role in shaping occupational risks, one's social position prior to entry into sex work is crucial in determining one's occupational experiences.

Theoretical Foundations

My approach to the health of sex workers in this book has been shaped primarily by social science scholarship on women's health, particularly those approaches that emphasize the impact of political economy, structural violence, social geography, gender, and social change.[4] The majority of these scholars are anthropologists (and critical medical anthropologists, more specifically) who have applied their approach to understanding structural risk for HIV/AIDS infection. The framework used by critical medical anthropologists "emphasizes the importance of political and economic forces, including the exercise of power, in shaping health, disease, illness experience, and health care" (Singer and Baer 1995: 5). These contributions demonstrate the interconnectedness of the biological with social, political, and economic processes, forcing one to move beyond the medical gaze in understanding health and illness toward an understanding of health disparities and social justice.

The *intersectionality* paradigm has also been a significant underlying framework of this book. The theory of intersectionality works to highlight the multiple and interconnected ways in which subordination affects women's experiences, their help-seeking behaviors, and their ability to manage the risks in their lives. For example, researchers have examined the multiple structural oppressions faced by victims and survivors of intimate partner violence, and they have explored as well the question of agency in the face of multiple forms of oppression (Connell 1997; Crenshaw 1994). While the threat of male violence may exist for all women, it is only one aspect of the systemic subordination experienced by, for example, poor women of color. Poverty and racism compound both the experience of physical abuse and women's ability to receive the support needed to leave abusive situations or to hold their partners accountable for the abuse they have inflicted. In a move away from a hegemonic feminism that universalizes women's experiences of gendered subordination, many feminist scholars now attend to the complex interrelationships between gendered subordination, racial discrimination, and economic deprivation. It is this framework that sets the foundation for understanding the multidimensional relationship between individuals' position within the sex work hierarchy, their differential exposure to occupational risk, and their capacity to successfully manage those risks in everyday life.

In the hierarchy of sex work, gender, race, and class are not the only social forces impacting the experiences of individual sex workers. Legal status, age, work site, and language skills also shape work experiences by filtering the kinds of customers they may come into contact with, the kinds of working conditions they may have to deal with, and the relationships they might have with health inspectors, clinic staff, and police. Occupational risks are not distributed evenly. And the ability to deal successfully with occupational hazards depends on one's position in the hierarchy and the kinds of resources one has at hand.

Because of the high degree of social diversity within the sex industry and the lack of basic research on sex work in Mexico, this book was especially challenging to write. In an effort to encompass the broad range of sex workers' experiences in Tijuana and to illustrate links between their personal narratives and practices and the larger social environment of which they are a part, I attempt to capture a range of experiences within the sex industry and to make sense of how work experiences are related to one's social background. I include personal narratives in order to detail how commercial sex workers navigate and negotiate their everyday work lives; these subjective understandings are contextualized within more quantitative data on health outcomes related to work activities. Along the way, I also suggest structural interventions—that is, interventions that go beyond the realm of individual behavior and into the realm of policy, law, and other reforms—that could facilitate positive health behaviors and outcomes by reducing social constraints.

Outline of the Book

In chapter 1 I briefly outline the origins of commercial sex work along the border. From the early colonial period onward, residents of the Tijuana–San Diego region have utilized class and race relations to establish a commercialized sex industry and govern sexual relations. Unequal relations between the United States and Mexico have allowed the United States to practice a policy of containment that repeatedly attempts to discourage vice on one side of the border (the United States), while allowing the vice industry on the other side of the border to flourish.

In chapter 2 I examine the role of rapid urbanization, border migration, and structural inequality in furthering the expansion of the Tijuana sex industry. Understanding the sex industry within the context of the shifting political economy of the border helps one develop a more general understanding of the relationship between health and social change as well as of the position of the sex industry in relation to other contemporary social and economic features. For example, the global assembly line, in which the manufacturing industry employs a spatial strategy at the international level to generate increased profits, has had a tremendous impact in drawing young women and girls to the border in search of factory employment. Discouraged by low wages, long hours, sexual harassment, lack of advancement opportunities, and the rising cost of living, some of these new residents leave the factory to engage in sex work, adding to the already plentiful supply of commercial sex workers. Human trafficking and sexual slavery, both of which are encouraged by structural inequalities between the United States and Mexico and facilitated by conditions on the border, also play a role in generating supply and demand of sexual services on both sides of the border. Although none of the participants in this study reported a history of sexual slavery, the relationship of human sexual trafficking and other forms of trafficking to the rest of the industry is too important to be overlooked.

Although their options are limited by the structural violence of material constraints, poverty, lack of education, and gender-based discrimination, those who engage in sex work continue to act within these constraints in an effort to improve their quality of life. In chapter 3 I explore, through their own words, the ways in which my participants became familiar with and interested in commercial sex work. Although engaging in sex work negatively impacts one's sexual and social respectability, the reality of life in Tijuana, poverty, limited opportunities for economic advancement, partner abandonment, family responsibilities, and drug addiction create a context wherein sex work, which certainly carries very obvious physical and social risks, begins to make sense in relation to the available alternatives.

I continue in chapter 4 by illustrating the social and geographic contours of the industry, highlighting the role of policing and social stratification in shaping a social hierarchy that has a profound influence on how sex work activities are experienced and managed. I adduce specific details about the social geography of the industry, laying the groundwork for understanding the relationship between social relations and occupational health outcomes.

Fear of sex workers as vectors of sexually transmitted infection has led to calls for the increased regulation of sex workers via registration, mandatory testing, and criminal penalties. Though this system is intrusive, compliance can benefit workers in the formal system. Illegal workers, however, face added risk as a result of their legal status. Thus, in chapter 5 I present the intricacies of the regulation system in Tijuana and consider how policing strategies affect occupational risk for violence, mental health problems, and STIS, including HIV/AIDS. In particular, I compare the differing risks faced by legal and illegal workers and discuss how the police mitigate or, in the case of illegal workers, increase occupational risks. This regulatory framework shapes not only the occupational risks faced by sex workers, but also the social organization of sex work more generally as well as the particular place of a sex worker within the commercial sex hierarchy, the ability to claim a more professional social status, and the likelihood of transcending highly stratified class lines. Last, I profile those female sex workers who tested positive for HIV in this study and examine how one might understand their risk for HIV infection in light of these findings.

In chapter 6 I discuss the effects of gender in defining the experiences of individual sex workers. I present a discussion of narratives on stigma, mental health, and drug addiction to deepen understanding of this process and help address the special needs of female, male, and transgender sex workers within this system. I pay particular attention to the role of gender in organizing sexual and drug-related risk for HIV/AIDS.

In the conclusion, I summarize the major findings of my research in Tijuana and the role of law and policy in shaping occupational health and safety. I then identify the specific problems with the Tijuana regulatory model and examine these findings in light of the debates surrounding sex work and the law. Finally, I explore how these policies might be reimagined in order to better address sex workers' occupational health.

Methodology

It was not until I had been living in Tijuana for a number of months that I realized how structurally diverse the commercial sex industry is. My goal of writing a purely qualitative study shifted as I began to strategize about how to incorporate this diversity and, more specifically, to identify patterns in the relationships between social diversity, social hierarchy, and health outcomes. In order to capture a multiplicity of experiences and perspectives from different points within the sex work hierarchy, I used a combination of participant observation, informal conversational interviews, semistructured interviews, and surveys conducted in a variety of settings. The use of targeted, purposive sampling allowed me to explore potential themes within a broad range of diverse work experiences. I talked with customers, professionals, researchers, and policymakers[5]—but I collected the most extensive data from talking with sex workers themselves. In all, I carried out 251 formal interviews with sex workers, 88 of whom worked legally (86 females, 2 transgendered females), and 160 of whom worked illegally (107 females, 14 transgendered females, 42 males).

Potential subgroups of sex workers were identified through my own observational research and conversations as well as through my familiarity with other research on sex workers in other cities. The subgroups differ in terms of occupational experiences and risks, treatment by city officials and policy, gender and sexual orientation, and educational, class, and regional backgrounds. The majority of research on sex workers has focused on one subgroup to the exclusion of others (that is, males or females, strippers or hookers) with the majority of research studies focusing on female street hooking. In this study, I targeted a range of subgroups[6] with respect to their work venue (strippers, brothel workers, street hookers, massage parlor workers, call services). See the accompanying early dendogram, or tree diagram, that I created based on locale and work venue.

Participant Observation

I lived for eighteen months in Tijuana observing the commercial sex scene in Zona Norte, the red light area closest to the U.S.–Mexico border, Avenida Revolución, the most prominent tourist area, and the beaches and parks in Las Playas de Tijuana, a popular cruising and hooking area for men who have sex with men. What does participant observation mean in the study of the sex industry? Although some researchers have relied on their own sexual experiences or participation in a sexual arena (Bolton 1995; Carrier 1999) or commercial sex venue (Frank 2002) to gather data, I did not participate in the sex industry as either a client or a sex worker. I did, however, participate in the social life of people involved in the industry and in that of some of their customers. These informal conversations usually took place outside of the work venue and were very important when I first arrived in the field and was trying to get my bearings. They also helped me revise my survey questions, identify recruitment areas, and discuss my findings. I was straightforward about my intention to study the local sex industry, garnering many interested questions and commentary from local residents. Although many were reluctant to disclose their activities and a few never openly acknowledged their role in the sex industry, fear and mistrust about the project seemed to wane after time.

Semistructured Interviews

After obtaining informed consent, I collected 53 interviews with sex workers at the city clinic. These case studies provided preliminary details about the experiences of 50 female and 3 transgender sex workers who worked legally and received services from the clinic.[7] It soon became clear that the sex workers I

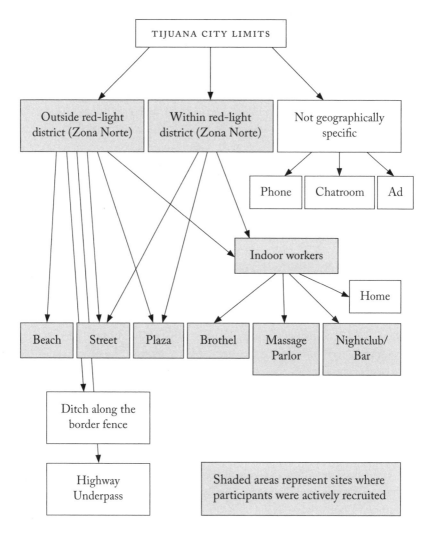

was speaking with represented only a small portion of the population of sex workers in Tijuana. This forced me to develop a more complex research design based on the local social organization of the industry. Even though the interviews were collected systematically, some areas within the interview schedule are covered more extensively with some participants than with others. Some included narrative data on areas perceived as significant to a handful of participants or to an individual participant, but not relevant to other participants. Also, as is commonly the case with qualitative data collection, I made constant revisions to the interview schedule, including new lines of inquiry as they emerged. The first set of interviews is therefore different from the last set, making statistical comparisons unfeasible. The interviews, which were carried out in Spanish, ran from one to two hours in length. In compensation for their time, I provided all participants with HIV/AIDS counseling, snacks, and refreshments as well as a copy of my research findings (in Spanish), made available through the clinic. All interviews were confidential and took place over a period of two months, April and May of 2001.

Surveys

After working in Tijuana for about six months, I received a grant from the National Science Foundation which allowed me to expand my study to include survey data and HIV-antibody testing.[8] My survey instrument included both closed and open-ended questions. After obtaining informed consent, the interviews were conducted in private locations near work sites or in a local café. Occasionally, the interviews were interrupted by potential customers. Each interview was conducted in Spanish and was approximately an hour long. All interviews and HIV tests were confidential. In compensation for their time, all participants received five dollars and refreshments, HIV/AIDS prevention information and counseling, an HIV-antibody test using Orasure, and, when applicable, referrals to public services. The provision of HIV testing undoubtedly encouraged participation in the study, as free, reliable, and confidential HIV testing and counseling were not widely available.[9] The basic demographic distribution of this survey sample is shown in the accompanying chart. The survey data presented are not representative of the entire population of sex workers in Tijuana. However, these data allowed me to capture the diversity of occupational experiences and practices among sex workers in Tijuana and to make comparisons among workers based on legal status, gender, and sexual orientation. This is highly important because there are no comprehensive or comparative studies on the sex industry in Tijuana. In my study, I found the ratio of those working illegally to those working legally to be approximately two to one. The actual proportion of workers in each sector is unknown. As mentioned previously, because this study started in a clinical setting with legal workers, the number of those working legally is not representative of the total number out in the real world. In addition, although legal workers were not targeted for inclusion in the survey phase of the project, they were not excluded from participating if they asked to do so. In some cases, they were peer leaders whose participation encouraged the participation of less experienced illegal workers. In others, they were enthusiastic, curious,

Survey Participant Characteristics (N=198)

Literacy
Read/Write Spanish (96%)
Speak English (27%)

Education
Elementary School (25%)
Junior High School (37%)
High School (25%)
University (2%)
Trade School (4%)

Gender
Female (70%)
Male (21%)
Transgender (8%)
Post-operative T. (1)
Pre-operative T. (7)
Transvestite (7)

Civil Status
Single (56%)
Cohabitating (23%)
Separated (7%)
Married (6%)
Divorced (8%)

Children
No children (40%)
At least one child (60%)
2–3 children (28%)
4–5 children (7%)

Sexual Orientation
Heterosexual (71%)
Bisexual (10%)
Gay (14%)
Lesbian (0%)

or desirous of a free, reliable HIV test. Their contributions offer an important contrast to the experiences of those working illegally.

After collecting these surveys, I used NUD*IST ethnographic software to combine narrative data from field notes, semistructured interviews, and surveys.[10] Numeric survey data were assessed and analyzed with SPSS and were then contextualized through narrative data.

CHAPTER ONE

Tijuana's Origins

*American culture values progress. We seem to believe that new is better, and
as a nation, we seem to think that progress is our most important product. We
expect most change to be improvement, which means, most of the time, increased
production, profits, and material possessions. As a society we are rich, but in what
ways are we better off?*
(BARLETT AND BROWN 1985: 25)

Long before Las Vegas emerged from the desert as a glittering haven for
gambling and sex work, Tijuana, Mexico, had established itself as a frontier
version of Sin City. Located on the western hemisphere's only first world/
third world border, Tijuana is estimated to be the busiest international border
crossing in the world (Ganster 1999). Like its border cousins, Ciudad Juárez
and, on a smaller scale, Nogales, Mexico, Tijuana draws from a vast network
of migrant labor, college students, tourists, and the U.S. armed services in providing demand for sex work labor at the border. In Tijuana, for example, fifty-
five million northward-bound migrants and tourists from the United States
flow through the city each year (ibid.). Because of its proximity to San Diego,
Los Angeles, and other West Coast cities, Tijuana is also a popular crossing ground for those who come from as far away as China, Russia, and the
Middle East. Its geographic importance has stimulated substantial growth in
tourism, services, and manufacturing. In its thriving transnational diversity
and as a major contender in the globalized manufacturing sphere, Tijuana is a
postmodern city and tourist mecca. The city welcomes the world's consumers
with open shops, restaurants, and night clubs. Tijuana caters to young and old,
and its downtown streets pulsate with music, voices, and laughter. The city
supplies need fulfillment on every level: food, beer, liquor, voyeurism, sex, and

recreation. Yet it remains a place that is virtually untouched, ethnographically speaking, until now.

The story of Tijuana goes beyond its current demographics, containing a variety of seemingly unrelated elements, from *sombreros* and *serapes* in the 1920s to sex tourism to televisions and the decline of the contemporary family farm. Combined, these factors form the patchwork quilt of supply and demand for the sex industry in Tijuana. Many facets of the political economy of the border have shaped the industry one finds today, from the macroeconomic forces shaping immigration to today's increasingly globalized sexual landscape.

Creating the U.S.-Mexico Border

From the beginning, social relations along the U.S.-Mexico border were formed through social inequity:

> The creation of the U.S.-Mexican boundary is best understood as a long historical process that began in the sixteenth century when England, Spain, and France competed for control of North America and that ended in the mid-nineteenth century when the United States absorbed large portions of the Mexican northern frontier through annexation, warfare, and purchase. . . . Americans now had a vast domain that extended from coast to coast, substantially boosting internal and external trade. The Mexican cession also yielded additional fertile lands and abundant gold, silver, copper, and other valuable resources. Thus, for both nations the making of the boundary proved to be a determining factor in their development. (Martinéz 1996: 1)

The boundary line ensured that the United States would remain resource rich, while still in a position to extract labor resources from south of its border. This asymmetry continues to characterize the border today.

Early Northward Migrations

The planned use of labor from south of the border began in the latter part of the nineteenth century, when employers in the United States were actively seeking inexpensive labor to support economic growth, especially in the newly emerging American Southwest (Cockcroft 1986). This labor force was involved in agribusiness, cattle, felling trees, mining ore, and laying down railroads. Despite fluctuations in the U.S. economy, the number of workers from Mexico and Central America that are employed in the United States has increased with every successive generation:

> Mexican labor became fundamental for the development, survival, growth of much U.S. agribusiness, as well as for the garment and electronics industries, select sectors of heavy industry such as automotive and steel, and the restaurant, hotel, and other service industries. Today, the substantial presence of Mexicans in an ever-expanding and ever more international reserve army of labor facilitates economic recovery and potential expansion for industry as a whole. (Cockcroft 1986: 217)

From 1940 to the mid-1960s, the residents of Tijuana were inundated by Mexican migrants drawn by the growing agricultural industry of the Southwest. American immigration policies such as the *bracero* program and the revolving door of guest worker visas have acted as a strong incentive pulling migrants from central and southern Mexico into the United States through the Tijuana corridor.

Early Vice Tourism

During the 1920s and 1930s Tijuana was a hot spot for movie stars, celebrities, and tourists. Racetracks, casinos, dance halls, breweries, and brothels thrived south of the border, which benefited from prohibitionist reform movements in the United States. By 1919, the Los Angeles and San Diego Railroads connected Tijuana to the main arteries of the United States, which facilitated development of a local entertainment industry. The building of two new military bases in southern California represented a boon to the local economy—a large population of mostly unattached male consumers who to this day visit Tijuana for R and R (rest and relaxation).

Business operators in southern California, forced out of business because of the Volstead Act of 1919, which federally mandated alcohol prohibition, quickly established Tijuana as the site that provided entertainment and services not legal or affordable in the United States. "Any thirsty San Diegan could hop in his Model T and be in a legal Tijuana bar within half an hour. Here he could drink the finest Scotch and Brandy available" (SDHS 2002a: 115). Tijuana also served as the most popular illicit distributor for the finest speakeasies in San Diego:

While there were plenty of speakeasies in town, the "bon ton" went to the Studio Club at Sixth and Juniper. A turreted pile of old sandstone, the building had been decorated lavishly with richly carved woods and stain-glass windows. The fixtures in the bathrooms were gold-plated. The host was a gentleman by the name of Dave Wrotenberg and he was never bothered by the police. The fact that City Council members held ex-officio meetings weekly in one of the private rooms may have had something to do with this state of affairs. Dave could boast that his product was pure. He should know. He made it himself. Into a five-gallon charred keg went two gallons of 180-proof alcohol made in Tijuana, three gallons of water, a jigger of glycerin, and Kitchen Bouquet for color. After ageing for three months, the mixture was ready for the average non-discriminating palate. (SDHS 2002a: 21)

Like many cities in the United States, especially those along major shipping routes, Tijuana tolerated a zoned area of sex work in the poorest part of the city:

> If, in the 1890's, there had been such a thing as a West Coast tourist guide book, San Diego would have rated five fat stars with the deep water sailors of the period. After a howling trip around Cape Horn, a ship would drop its hook in warm San Diego Bay, the crew would be paid, and every one of them would head for the "Stingaree" as fast as the ship's boats would carry them. (ibid.)

This neighborhood, known as the Stingaree, was similar to what one might have found in Tijuana during that period. Although it was disreputable and a source of embarrassment to reformers, city officials were reluctant to apply any legal pressure: "It is not my idea entirely to destroy the Stingaree and force its inmates all over the city, as I consider it best to district them. . . . I believe it will finally be necessary to shut up these temperance saloons and confine the women to less public quarters" (SDHS 2002b: 115). When the Stingaree was closed in 1912, it is said that the women were sent out of town on the railroad, followed by a "scraggly line of barkeeps, opium sellers, gamblers, runners, and panhandlers" (ibid.) — no doubt adding to the popularity of the brothels in Tijuana.

From the beginning, Tijuana brothels and strip shows became a normalized part of the local recreation industry, sold right along with tacos, beer, and the classic donkey photo.[1] Tijuana businesses invested in vice-based tourism for the pleasure of U.S. tourists. As in San Diego, efforts to "clean up" the city by cracking down on sex workers reveal a concern with the image of the

Figure 1.1. A T-shirt sold at the Chicago Club in 2003. The Chicago Club is one of the large strip-club brothels in the Zona Norte. The imagery of the club evokes the glamour of the vice industry during Prohibition.

city more than anything else. In 1991, tourist spending in Tijuana was an estimated seven hundred million dollars, twice that provided by the manufacturing sector (Ganster 1999). Like the Stingaree, the vice industry in Tijuana is tolerated, and as the largest contributor to the municipal tax base it is likely to stay that way. Downtown Tijuana is still characterized as a vice-ridden economy. It adds to its contemporary reputation by providing illegal street drugs, cheap pharmaceuticals without prescription, alcohol sales to minors, and a thriving sex trade—most of which is marketed directly to U.S. tourists, who have access to disposable income. The consumption of these products and services overlaps the more normative consumption of curios and agricultural products associated with Mexican culture.

CHAPTER TWO

Tijuana Today

Residents in the U.S.-Mexico border regions have overlapped economically, socially, and culturally for over 150 years. An estimated forty thousand residents of Tijuana travel to and from San Diego to work each day, spending an estimated one to three billion dollars on retail goods and services while in the United States (Lorey 1999). Family and social ties on both sides of the border remain strong, in spite of the increasing militarization of the border. Rural to urban and transnational ties continue to link migrants to their home communities, profoundly shaping their motivations, labor strategies, attitudes, and practices. By the 1980s the migrant population comprised nearly half of the total border population (Ganster 1999). More than any other factor, migration has shaped the demographic picture of the U.S.-Mexico border region.

In 1990, the Tijuana service sector employed about 53 percent of the working residents of Tijuana; the manufacturing sector employed the remaining 46 percent (ibid.). Only 35 percent of the workers in Tijuana are considered part of the formal economy. Those who work in the informal economy do not have Social Security benefits or subsidized health insurance and must rely on an underfunded public health care system that provides for only the most basic needs.[1]

The majority of residents in Tijuana are below the poverty line. About 30 percent of workers in Tijuana make one hundred dollars a month (fifty-two cents an hour); 10 percent make less (MSN 2002a). Less than 15 percent make enough money to shelter, feed, and clothe their families (ibid.). Very few have disposable income. In order to compensate for the lack of viable employment opportunities, over forty thousand residents commute to San Diego, where they are able to make about five hundred dollars a month (Ganster 1999). These workers make up Tijuana's small emerging middle class.

Figure 2.1. Southbound traffic into Tijuana. Lax border regulations allow free-flowing traffic into Mexico. The heaviest flows into Tijuana are at the end of the workday for commuters who work in San Diego and on weekends, when tourists flood the downtown area.

Contemporary Migration

The border acts as an escape valve; the departure of the large segments of the poor helps keep Mexico's government stable (Schatz 1998). According to a former mayor of Tijuana, "Mexico hasn't had a big social uprising because we have this escape valve[;] if there was no place to go, they'd have to make a solution here" (Parfit 1996: 105).

Today, Tijuana is a city of just over one million residents, over 56 percent of whom are recent arrivals from southern Mexico (Ganster 1999). An estimated 20 percent are not permanent residents, and over fifty thousand are in transit to the United States. Contrary to popular fears of illegal immigration, only 1 percent of travel over the border into the United States is done illegally. About 25 percent of the city population is considered a floating population; they are not permanent residents of Tijuana and are in transit to and from the United States. The northward migratory flow is based on incentives found in the United States, including jobs in agribusiness, construction, domestic, hotel, and restaurant services. This flow ensures cheap, if not always legal, labor, which increases profits and keeps costs low for consumers. Migrant workers are able to make more money in the United States than at home, but most must leave their families for long periods of time in order to do so.

The vast majority of migrants work in the United States not just because it is an attractive option, but because they are unable to make ends meet at home. According to the Mexican secretary of social development, more than half of all Mexicans live in poverty, making less than $1.50 per day in rural areas and $2.10 in its cities (MSN 2002a). One quarter do not have enough to eat. Since the 1990s, an additional 4.7 million Mexicans live in extreme poverty, comprising 52.6 percent of the population in 1992, and 69.6 percent after 1995 (ibid.). Today, poverty levels are close to 65 percent, and in 2002, another 1.3 million Mexicans fell below the poverty line (ibid.).

In rural areas, more than 70 percent live in poverty (MSN 2002b). The decreased quality of life in rural areas is directly connected to commercial open-

Figure 2.2. The "Mall." Mexican curio vendors wait for the throngs of tourists to arrive. Tourist foot traffic is channeled through this area before crossing the Tijuana River to get downtown.

Figures 2.3a, b. Vendors at the San Ysidro border crossing (northbound). Curio vendors hawk their wares to motorists traveling back to the United States. Waits of up to two or three hours encourage a healthy business.

ings and to free trade under the agricultural policies of the administration of former president Vicente Fox. Local producers have been unable to compete with heavily subsidized U.S. farmers in the globalized marketplace. Although the Mexican government has promised subsidies to local farmers, they have not yet arrived. In 2003, as a result of the continuing removal of tariffs on agricultural imports, an estimated five million *campesinos* (peasants) migrated northward to the United States (MSN 2002c). Those who are unable to cross the international boundary provide the labor pool for the tourist, service, and manufacturing sectors, which comprise 99 percent of the city's gross regional product (Ganster 1999).

Manufacturing Industry

Since the 1960s, a growing manufacturing industry has encouraged a variety of international agreements, from the Programa Nacional Frontero (PRONAF) and the Border Industrialization Program (BIP) in the early 1960s to NAFTA in 1994 (Lorey 1999). With each program, tariffs and taxes on imports and exports have slowly been removed, increasing transnational capital flows throughout the United States, Canada, and Mexico.

Figure 2.4. Family picnic at the Playas de Tijuana. A "cross-border" family shares a summer picnic through the fence. A small permanent passway allows food to be shared on both sides of the international border.

Drawn by cheap labor, thousands of *maquiladoras*, or Mexican factories, built in the city have made Tijuana one of the world's largest centers of production for textiles, electronics, and foodstuffs: for example, Tijuana produces more television sets than any other city in the world (Parfit 1996: 107). The majority of new industries are dominated by foreign capital under the auspices of corporations like Ford, General Electric, Sanyo, and Mitsubishi. Local workers have been largely unable to capitalize on developments in manufacturing because of their low household income and the inflated cost of living along the border.

Following a neoliberal approach imposed by the World Bank and the International Monetary Fund,[2] the Mexican government has spent what little money it does have on roads and airstrips for big industry rather than on water, sewage, and housing for the millions of workers who have flocked to the border area.[3] Some might frame the devastation caused by development as growing pains, implying that the devastation is repairable and temporary, but this paradigm ignores what dependency theorists have tried so diligently to bring to the public consciousness for nearly three decades, namely, that the development of large-scale economies such as that found in the United States requires the underdevelopment of others. Critics of the modernization paradigm frame development as a dependency-creating mechanism and a tool of imperialism (Escobar 1995). Nowhere is this more clear than in Tijuana.

Northward migration toward the United States and toward the money to be made along its border has meant rapid urbanization of border cities like Tijuana and the ensuing creation of microenvironments characterized by an extremely poor quality of life. In most habitable areas, the northern edge of the city is built right up to the border fence, "like children with noses to the window, all longing to be on the other side" (Parfit 1996: 97). The U.S. side tends to keep its distance from the fence, unwilling to confront the need on the other side.

Increasing militarization of the border and tighter control over work visas have trapped some migrants in Tijuana, which has become a catchment area for migrants who are often isolated, displaced, and destitute.[4] Border crossers can be seen at any time of the day or night along the three miles of fence; some nap while waiting for the cover of darkness, and others test newly made holes while keeping an eye out for the patrol on the other side.

Figure 2.5. Highway sign on Interstate 5 in California. The sign warns highway drivers that men, women, and children might run across the Interstate as they flee across the border.

Figure 2.6. Crossing the fence. Loved ones place crosses in honor of the dead who tried to cross the border. Many crosses bear the name and date of those who died, while even more show only the date, having been placed for someone unknown.

Sex Work versus Factory Work

Sex work appeals to the poor in a way that factory work cannot. First, unlike factory work in the United States, which pays a living wage, factory work in Mexico, which pays about fifty-two cents an hour on average, barely meets subsistence needs on the border. Seen from a rural area in the south, the wage might seem attractive, but the cost of living along the border is much higher than in other parts of Mexico.

Additionally, Mexican unions have not met with the same success as those in the United States, and factory work provides few opportunities for mobility, especially for women. Factory floor employees, for example, make about five to ten dollars a day and are expected to work five to seven days a week and about ten hours per shift (Peña 1997). They neither receive paid overtime, paid vacations, or paid holidays, nor do they have health insurance. A few can aspire to becoming a shift supervisor, but management is nearly exclusively male. The majority, therefore, cannot expect to climb the social ladder by accepting an entry-level position and working hard to secure a better-paying position in the future. Nearly all available positions are entry level, workers are easily and quickly replaced, there is little job security, and workers are often replaced if they call in sick to work. Labor organizing is sometimes met with violent intimidation. Unlike sex workers, factory workers cannot plan their days or evenings according to child care, family, or personal needs. They barely make enough to survive (many pool their factory wages in the household to pay for food and shelter), much less to save up for a vacation or to have a savings account. Health care, if not available in the factory location itself, is generally provided through volunteers and public services. Investment in a home takes years, rather than months, as many are not able to purchase an existing home.

Occupation-related violence and sexual harassment of women in Tijuana are not confined to sex workers, as other workers, especially factory workers, face similar risks at work and on their way to and from work. Traveling through the *colonias populares* (neighborhoods) located on the periphery of the city limits, especially after work in the dark, is so dangerous that police will not enter the areas to patrol or investigate criminal activities. According to local residents I spoke with in one neighborhood, the police do not track criminal activities in these neighborhoods and therefore have no records. The feeling among these residents was that the rape and murder of women as they walk from the maquiladora bus lines to their homes in the neighborhood are common. Most of these squatter-like settlements, which are built in the hills surrounding the city, just past the large industrial parks, lack potable water, sewage disposal, and electricity. They are not as established as neighborhoods found nearer the center of the city, which have, over time, built the necessary infrastructure to make their neighborhoods more habitable.

As Ward (1999) reminds us, *colonias populares* are common in Mexico because of the pressure that rapid urbanization and limited purchasing power put on local infrastructure. These neighborhoods are built on "an informal but widely recognized system of illegal sales and invasions . . . within the limitations of scarce public investment . . . and patron-client politics" (Heyman and Campbell 2004: 214). Although viewed primarily as a public health hazard by those in the United States, one is reminded that these neighborhoods are as much a solution as they are a problem (ibid.). Founded upon the initiative of people who have a desire to improve their situations but lack the resources needed to live in more established neighborhoods, these areas are home to many residents who work long hours to become more established. Each piece of a house—the foundation, walls, doors, and windows—is purchased and

Figures 2.7a, b. Border fence in Las Playas de Tijuana. Protesting the increasing militarization of the border and the deaths caused as a result of these policies, residents put up a message which reads, "Alto a Guardian" (Stop [Operation] Guardian). Each letter contains skulls with the first names of people who have died trying to cross into the United States.

installed bit by bit over time and with much pride. Some go up more quickly than others; it is common to see a brick and cement dwelling next to one made of metal sheeting and cardboard.

Life in these neighborhoods could be considered an environmental risk rather than an occupational one; however, it is related to occupational risks for two reasons. Factory workers, who can rarely afford their own transportation, need to live locally in order to stay employed at the factory, which provides transportation to and from their neighborhoods. Factories are increasingly being built further into the periphery, where land is cheap and plentiful as well as located near the airport and highway system. Additionally, the wages earned by factory workers prohibit them from living in less dangerous areas with access to more public services. Most families require multiple household wage earners in order to buy food as well as basic shelter.

Factory work has its own risks of sexual violence and harassment by supervisors and management. Litigation is virtually unheard of, as employees rarely make public claims against their superiors. They have no enforced protections and won't take the risk. Often, the workers are illegally employed minors who would lose their job were they to speak out. Several sex workers told me they decided to become sex workers precisely because of the level of violence and

Figure 2.8. 1st St. and Revolución. To the left, tourist foot traffic is directed up Revolución and away from Zona Norte by orange concrete barriers. Locals and *migrantes* sit idly, socializing, drinking, waiting to go to work or hook up with a *pollero* (smuggler) who will take them over the border.

harassment from factory supervisors or in their neighborhood. They further explained that they might as well get paid for being used as a sexual object, and that they would have done anything to escape those neighborhoods. The longer I lived in Tijuana, the more their choice to stay out of these neighborhoods made sense to me. The decision to become a sex worker is a sensible, calculated choice made within a setting that provides few alternatives for an enhanced quality of life. It is, in short, a decision to survive and even, in some ways, to thrive.

Migration into and through Tijuana has created a population explosion and brought with it a pace of urbanization that has far outstripped its resources. In 1930, the population of Tijuana was about eleven thousand (Lorey 1999). It grew to about five million in seventy years, the majority of that growth occurring in the last few decades of the twentieth century. Tijuana now has an estimated 6.75 percent annual population growth rate. Many people who move to Tijuana do so to get jobs in the maquiladoras:

They found that though maquiladora jobs were plentiful, salaries were so low—about thirty-five to forty-five dollars for a forty-eight-hour week—and costs so high that they could not afford to pay rent or utilities. They lived, for the most part, as squatters in shacks constructed from tin, wood pallets, plastic sheets, and cardboard boxes salvaged from the factories and the dump. Few had indoor plumbing; some had no water or electricity. Crime, disease, and family breakdown were rampant in the squatters' camps. But it was a reflection of the depth of poverty in Mexico that most of these workers felt they were better off [on the border] than they were in their hometown. (Davidson 2000: 11)

Faced with a municipal budget of just over fifty-three million dollars, Tijuana is unable to meet the demands of its growing population (Ganster 1999). Although some areas of Tijuana look like those of any U.S. city, with up-scale apartments, shopping malls, restaurants, museums, plazas, and lush golf courses, city development has been uneven. In poorer areas, residents face a host of health concerns which affect their quality of life, including malnu-

Figure 2.9. In front of the border gate to the United States. A business owner waits for customers who will pay for bus rides to cities along the migration route.

Figures 2.10a, b. Residential streets in Playas de Tijuana. Trash and open sewage can be seen all over Tijuana, even in middle-class residential areas with piped water and trash collection. A large transient population, stray dogs, and visitors make it difficult to keep the area clean.

trition, contaminated food and water, diarrheal disease, tuberculosis, heavy air pollution, industrial waste, accidents, lack of adequate shelter, and violence. The following infrastructure deficiencies have yet to be addressed (ibid.):

- Education: Students spend six years in school on average, and only 54.3 percent of students receive postprimary schooling;
- Air pollution: Poorly maintained vehicles, continued use of leaded fuel, traffic congestion, uncontrolled burning of solid waste, factory solvents, dust from unpaved streets, fecal dust from open sewage, sulfur clouds from the thermoelectric plant, and polluted air from Los Angeles and San Diego;
- Traffic: Traffic congestion and deterioration of roads due to heavy factory-related truck and border traffic; average commute to and from work is two hours; many areas lack paving; 50 percent of paved roads need repair;
- Housing: Land invasions into unstable, hilly areas susceptible to flooding and landslides as well as property disputes;

- Water and electricity: 15 percent of residents in the *colonias* (literally "neighborhoods" but used to refer to peri-urban areas surrounding the city) lack electricity and potable water; all residents lack access to contamination-free piped water; water delivery trucks, filling stations, and bottled water are available at high cost;
- Sewage: Most *colonias* lack sewer systems; residents use pit privies and hillsides, which leads to renegade sewage flows during storms, and widespread contamination of running and standing water;
- Hazardous waste: Close proximity to industrial and residential areas; illegal hazardous waste dumped into *colonia* neighborhoods runs down roads and into homes during winter rains;
- Infant mortality: 26.9 per 1,000, four times that in neighboring San Diego;
- Water-born disease: Gastrointestinal diseases, hepatitis, and other diseases transmitted by impure water.

In order to curb the growth of prostitution along the border, the structural and economic issues faced by residents must be successfully dealt with. The political economy of the border and the role of the United States in shaping that landscape must be acknowledged. The United States and Mexico share a

border over three thousand miles in length, and they must also bear responsibility for limiting the negative consequences of their actions.

Social Environment

Migration displaces people from social networks and social resources found at home. They are not only isolated from their family, friends, and primary sexual partners, but also lack access to legal and political representation, health services, and education. In Tijuana, most sex workers are migrants themselves, serving a customer base which is also largely made up of migrant workers.

Constant, rapid migration to and through Tijuana has also shaped the social environment of the city. Although there are certainly some quieter, gentrified areas of the city, I would describe the social environment I found in Tijuana as one rife with social chaos: rumors of corruption (usually well founded), visible street violence against residents, city officials, tourists, and rival drug gangs, hustling, hawking, fear, distrust, and suspicion as well as an ardent tenacity to get ahead. The lack of permanence that is pervasive and real in Tijuana is not only socially disruptive, but also discourages personal and social investment in local community networks, community organizing, and community-based interventions.

When combined with the alienating experience of migration to urban areas, and the particular impact of globalization on the U.S.-Mexico border, it is not surprising that for commercial sex workers, issues of daily survival, the continual pressures of poverty, marginalization, and exploitation, and the desire for socioeconomic mobility may outweigh the perceived relevance of potential risk for sexually transmitted infections (STIs). The perceived importance of STIs is exacerbated by the nature of STIs like syphilis, gonorrhea, and AIDS, which have long latency periods and confusing, disparate symptoms. However, the long-term effects of STIs and the rising morbidity and mortality rates among sexually active youth make research on STI risk and prevention fundamental to the improvement of quality of life.

CHAPTER THREE

Milk Money, Drug Money, and the Sexual Entrepreneur

I did not have the money for my daughter's milk.

GUADALUPE

Milk money, drug money, and the sexual entrepreneur are three loosely defined categories that describe the motivations cited by the majority of participants in this study for engaging in sex work. They would probably apply in nearly any setting, in different proportions depending on economic climate, employment opportunities, welfare services, drug treatment services, and the like. In Tijuana, most of the sex workers I met fell into the milk money category, focusing on the provision of basic needs for themselves and their children (see table 3.1 for a general overview of primary motivations for entering sex work). Others used commercial sex work as a form of entrepreneurship and socioeconomic mobility, a way to send their family to college, to invest in small business ventures, to save money toward home ownership, or to acquire luxury goods and social status. Drug addiction was not the primary motive for entry into sex work for the sex workers involved in this study. Guadalupe, age twenty-seven, was born in Sinaloa, Mexico. She attended school through the sixth grade, at which time she dropped out to help supplement the family's household income. A woman with two young children to raise and no male partner to support her, Guadalupe was forced to rely on jobs in the informal economy to make ends meet. She received no support from her parents, as her father had moved away from the family home when she was three years old and her mother operated a small street-side vendor operation that generated barely enough money to put food on the table. Because Guadalupe wanted her children to attend school, she was highly motivated to work in spite of the compromises she would have to make on the job. Holding down a job

Table 3.1. Primary Route into Sex Work (by Gender) (percentages)

	Female	*Male*	*Trans*
Advertisement	39	5	—
Friend also does sex work	36	32	57
Propositioned by a stranger	9	58	29
Workplace opportunities	7	5	7
Family member a sex worker	6	—	7
Partner	3	—	—

while having two children to support is next to impossible for many. Even in the United States, which has social services available to the poor, this is a difficult endeavor. In Mexico, where there is no welfare system in place to provide financial assistance, housing assistance, and assistance with day care, there are few options, even for those with job skills and an education. Many move to the border area to work in factory jobs for up to fifty hours a week, earning about forty dollars a week, nowhere near enough to support a family on a single income. Factory jobs are among the best-paid jobs for the working class but have little job security and few, if any, benefits.

Looking at the limited options available to women who want or need to be economically independent, I am always struck by how many *don't* engage in commercial sex work—a better question for future study might be why some women don't choose sex work over other options, given the stark contrast in earned income and the scheduling flexibility that is so important to a woman with children. Why would a woman choose to labor in a potentially risky environment, where she can be exposed regularly to industrial waste and toxins, sexual harassment, and long work hours when she can make in one hour what factory employees make in a week? When I asked Guadalupe how she got started working in the sex industry, she responded,

I did not have a job. [Some of my friends] told me that you could earn well here [in Tijuana]. And I came over here all by my little self. I had worked at three pool halls but the owners always wanted me to drink with the customers, and one time they put something in my drink and the owner raped me. Later, a man who was a customer at a restaurant where I worked, gave me $300 pesos each time we went out and I decided it was better if I charged whatever I wanted. I needed money and I met a friend who told me there was a place where they earned money. A girlfriend who worked at a massage parlor told me you earned good money and they needed masseuses where she worked and since I needed money, I started to think and I said: "That is ok." A girlfriend of hers opened a massage parlor and invited me to work there. I just went to visit and that was it, I decided to do it and I stayed. I told a co-worker from my last job about the work massage parlor and we both started working here.

Guadalupe's narrative points to the significance of gaining a degree of personal control over living and working conditions, both prior to and as a consequence of entry into sex work. Although there is no typical profile of a sex worker, all sex workers have one thing in common: each expresses his or her degree of personal autonomy within a particular social environment, an environment that structures both their opportunities for and constraints against particular forms of action. Their personal experiences as sex workers are as diverse as the reasons they give for entering into and continuing commercial sexual exchange. Both their motivations for engaging in sex work and their experiences as sex workers are largely shaped by their individual frame of reference, their social location vis-à-vis others, their perceptions of various alternatives, and the social environment in which they are embedded. First, I will examine the primary motivating factors for entry into sex work and how the recruitment process works in Tijuana. I will discuss these factors generally at first and then illustrate how the experiences differ between female, male, and transgender sex workers.

The most common motivation for sex work among participants in this study was the desire to escape a low quality of life.[1] Some sex workers come from desperate situations, are in need of shelter and food, and live in an environment in which there are few social safety nets and no municipal- or government-funded social services. Others work to provide for their aging or disabled parents who have no resources (there is no welfare or disability system in Tijuana) or to pay for medical treatment, surgery, and medications for family members. Many stated that although they tried to find other forms of employment, they were unsuccessful because of specific barriers, such as a lack of documentation, lack of education or skills or both, physical disability, obesity, sexual orientation, or transgender status. The inability to find alternate employment was discussed often, especially by transgender workers, who were often discriminated against by potential employers. Addressing barriers to employment is an unmet need that could facilitate the utilization of alternatives to sex work.

Like any other worker, sex workers in Tijuana decide they are looking for a particular kind of job and then go get it. They are not forced to engage in sex work by pimps or caught in a vicious cycle of debt with a brothel owner. In fact, pimps are rare figures in the lives of sex workers in Tijuana.[2] The vast majority harbored no illusions about what sex work entailed when they started in the business; they simply needed money and were not able to get what they wanted or needed from another resource. Most of them have specific reasons for not being able to make ends meet: for example, they may be a single parent and have children to feed; they've been abandoned by a spouse or partner; they've been fired or laid off; they can't get a job because they lack the necessary skills, education, or documentation; they don't make enough money at their current job; they've had to leave home at an early age because of sexual or physical abuse or harassment; they're living on the street with no one to help provide for them; they're addicted to drugs or crave a glamorous lifestyle; they want to save for a house or car; they want to complete high school or get a vocational or college degree. For many, it's not just one reason but a combination of reasons that makes an alternative form of work unfeasible. After all, a skilled sex worker can make five times what the average professional worker can make, including business owners, professors, doctors, and city officials. And they can easily make ten times what the majority of residents in Tijuana make, including factory workers, domestics, receptionists, and service staff.

The temptation to get into sex work is strong, especially when one's friends, coworkers, or relatives are already involved or when one has already made a lifestyle choice to socialize with friends on the streets or in bars. Accepting a chance proposition when you are out of money for food or have no place to stay is pretty easy. And once in the life, it's hard to get out. For some, the lure of quick money is too strong to resist. Sex work begins to "make sense" as an option when seen in context, as a product of a combination of factors: growing familiarity and desensitization toward the industry, never-ending propositions by customers, wage differences, economic instability, and the unfulfilled desire for consumer-oriented activities and products.

Routes of Entry

The route of entry into sex work illustrates the level of agency involved in the work itself. For example, in recent years there have been a number of media accounts of sex slavery rings in the United States that bring women from Mexico with the promise of a good job and money to send home to family. Upon their arrival, their passports are confiscated, they are often drugged, and many are forced to engage in prostitution in suburban homes-turned-brothels. Most never see their earnings, which go immediately from customer to owner. Obviously, there is no real negotiating power in these situations, as victims risk injury to themselves or their families back home for noncompliance. Often, to prevent them from seeking help, U.S. authorities threaten them with imprisonment as well.

Although lies, threats, coercion, and force have been documented in many parts of the world (including along the U.S.-Mexico border), my participants' responses demonstrate that the majority of those participating in this study have been neither duped into this kind of work, nor coerced by strangers. While deceit, coercion, or parental complicity are almost certainly factors in particular segments of the industry, it is likely that I was not able to access these individuals for participation in my study. Thus, while I would hesitate to generalize about all Tijuana sex workers, this book does bring to light something that is often overlooked. While the participants' narratives about how they got started in the business highlight the decision-making process involved in their choosing sex work over other alternatives, they do not shed light on the very different experiences of sexual commerce had by those who are held captive by their employers.

The most common routes of entry are through friends (word of mouth) (37 percent) and newspaper advertisements (28 percent), followed by propositions by customers (see table 3.2). The route of entry into sex work is highly gendered. Whereas females are most likely to become involved through an advertisement, males are more likely to become involved after being propositioned. Transgender sex workers are most likely to get involved after hearing about the business from a friend. As I discuss in the following chapter on gender differences, routes of entry reflect the gendered nature of the commercial sexual landscape more generally, with female sex work taking place in a more commercialized, formal manner than that of male and transgender work.

Friendship and Family Networks

Forty-six percent of the sex workers I interviewed found out about the profession through friends and family. For the most part, friends and family don't act as professional recruiters for the industry, nor do they receive finder's fees, but they do act as a trusted source of information. This process can occur through word of mouth or through comments made by male or female friends. Sometimes potential recruits are encouraged to enter sex work by friends who themselves are already involved in it.

Table 3.2. Primary Motivation for Entry (by Gender) (percentages)

	Female	Male	Trans
Primary provider for family members	30	—	—
Unspecified	17	25	14
Peer/social network involved	1	33	43
Savings goals/financial investments	11	—	7
Family conflict/ran away from home	8	5	7
Unemployed/no other source of income	7	10	—
Low wages from other job	8	3	—
Living on the street	2	13	22
Seen as "easy money"	4	5	—
To support drug and/or alcohol addiction	6	3	—
To support educational costs	5	3	7

Similar processes occur with family members who are already in the business, which accounts for 5 percent of the routes of entry identified by participants. Generally, the family member is a cousin or sister, and the recruitment nearly always involves a female-female relationship (only one male and no transgender sex workers had learned about the trade from a relative). Having friends or relatives in the business normalizes entry into it. While it cannot erase the damage done by occupational hazards, including the loss of respectability and a personal sense of decency, the *normalization process* can mitigate the fear and anxiety involved in getting started in the business. The normalization process takes place in three additional arenas: exposure to the work through advertising, while in a related occupation, or through propositions by customers.

Newspaper Advertisements

The second most common route of entry for sex workers is the newspaper (28 percent). Newspaper advertisements for sex workers fill the want ad section of both local newspapers. The ads can be specific, as in the case of ads for massage parlor workers, or they may gloss over the sexual nature of the work, as in the case of ads looking for models, hostesses, escort services, etc. Recruitment ads are generally the largest, most eye-catching items in the section, and they promise fast, easy money in an amount that few companies can compete with.

Propositions by Customers

Eighteen percent of the participants in my study got started in the sex industry as a result of propositions by potential customers. Nearly all of those who entered through this route were male. Although entry into many segments of the female sex industry are fairly institutionalized, with women and younger girls actively seeking work in established venues, male and transgender workers often stumble upon a customer while engaging in everyday activities. These propositions can occur at unexpected moments, when shopping for groceries, walking through a park, working, hanging out, or waiting for a friend. Although male and transgender workers described being singled out as a boost to their self-esteem,[3] females were more likely to remember the experiences as disconcerting, objectifying, and even frightening.

Ricardo, who was nineteen at the time of the interview, was born in Tijuana. He was excluded from his family network because he was gay. Living on the streets with friends like himself, Ricardo was encouraged to start hanging out in parks, where he could make some money:

> I was walking through Teniente Guerrero Park when I was sixteen, a guy who was about 23 came over and invited me home with him, we had sex and he gave me some money and that is how I started going to the park. Usually, I would be hanging out with a small group [of gay kids] and clients would drive by and would leave with the one they liked. One time, I was walking through the park and an older guy called me over, we talked, he took me to his house and since I did not have money for a private taxi I asked him and he gave me money for the taxi and for me. [Another day] a man came over and told me on the street that if I let him fondle me that he would give me $50 dollars and since I needed money, I told him I would and we went to a hotel. Sometimes, I go to the Ranchero Bar [a popular gay hangout]. There are *gringos* [white Americans] there, and they send beers over and then they ask if we can go to the hotel. (Ricardo, nineteen, male sex worker)

His friend Juan was also propositioned in a park and later in the parking lot of a supermarket on the way home from a job as a parking attendant, where he made a few dollars a day:

> When I was living in Los Angeles, I skateboarded over to a park when I was sixteen. A gay man offered me money to let him suck me off and he gave me $30 dollars that I used to buy things for myself. Later, I was coming from

"Carnitas Uruapan" [a restaurant near the La Mesa area of Tijuana] and around 10th Street near the Calimax [supermarket] there was a gay [person] and he offered me money. I was in need and accepted. This was about seven or eight years ago. (Juan, twenty-three, male sex worker)

While male and transgender workers are typically propositioned for the first time in popular gay male cruising areas like the park or the beach, they also utilize fictive kin networks (where an older transgender helps a young person learn the ropes) to gain entry into indoor venues. Sometimes, having sex with the doorman can facilitate their entry into indoor venues that would otherwise be closed to them because of their age or gender status.

Commercial sex occurs in a framework of power dynamics based on age, gender, wealth, and nationality. It is this framework that customers sense when they make a proposition; they could not hope for a yes unless they've successfully identified someone as more vulnerable than themselves. The customer, as a consumer, shops for an item he would like to buy. As some customers describe it, it's like being a kid in a candy store. The process of a sexual transaction would not work as it does if the customer did not have something the potential sex worker wanted or needed. It is not just that the potential sex worker is poor, but that the customer has more than they do. In a city like Tijuana, which is known both for its sex industry and its poverty, the public spaces and the people who inhabit them are transformed into morally ambiguous objects, leading a more financially able customer to assume that he or she can safely proposition anyone without repercussions.[4]

Related Occupations

Seven percent of the sex workers in this study become familiar with and interested in sex work as a result of working in a related occupation. These related occupations are often not connected to sex work per se but are located within establishments where sex work is taking place. This is commonly the case with wait staff, receptionists, beauty salon operators, and hotel domestic staff in the red light area:

[I started] because I saw that you earned more money. Before I used to work as a cashier at clothing or shoe stores. I have been working at this for a year. I came to a massage parlor as a receptionist and I saw that the girls earned more money. One day the owner told me to get up the nerve and I did. (Candida, twenty-four, female sex worker)

I was asked to work as a receptionist at a beauty parlor where they had massage and I started to work as a receptionist, but all the clients who came in asked for me, and they [the management] explained what was going on, that you could earn a lot of money and I decided to do it. (Mónce, twenty-three, female sex worker)

When I came here [to Coahuila Alley] the first time I came to Tijuana, I sold hot dogs. Later I began to dance at a bar and to *fichar* [drink with clients for a kickback], and when business was slow, in the beginning, I did not want to go with clients, but little by little I decided to go. (Solymar, twenty-eight, female sex worker)

Exposure to sex work activities in this way is obviously connected to consistent exposure to customer propositions as well as to the awareness that one's own work doesn't pay as well as that of one's peers. The crossing-over process between quasi-sex work activities (*fichera* dancing, strip dancing, etc.) and sexual intercourse with customers is easily facilitated by the way the formal sector is set up. In many establishments, employees are not required to have sexual intercourse but do so on a case-by-case basis or only to fulfill specific needs:

I was working in a bar dancing and drinking with clients, what is called working on commission. Since I was drinking too much, I decided to do something else, and massage seemed like an easy way to earn money. I found out through the newspaper. (Elsa, twenty-nine, female sex worker)

I began as a dancer in a bar. Less than two years ago I started to work at this because the money at the bars diminished and it was not enough for my expenses. I tried it here because of a girlfriend who brought me and here I am. (Myra, thirty-two, female sex worker)

Workers who can move fluidly from quasi-sex work activities to actual intercourse with customers and then back again are not trapped in that lifestyle. Rather, occasional sex work facilitates the attainment of specific financial goals. These workers have the ability to be selective and to negotiate the terms of the sexual transaction in a way that those working full time cannot.

An individual's management of occupational risks starts when deciding where and how to work. There are positive financial benefits associated with sex work, and many justify their tolerance for risk on the job by making comparisons between sex workers and other kinds of work, or lack of work. In this context, the choice to engage in sex work should be seen as a risk management strategy which replaces one set of risks with another.

Motivations

Poverty, Unemployment, and Being a Family Provider

In order to further understand how the sex worker labor pool is created, I collected narrative responses about why my participants chose sex work instead of other kinds of work. Then, as I did with the other data, I categorized the responses thematically, coding them and measuring them, until I had a clearer understanding of what kinds of things motivated these sex workers to take up sex work. In all my initial conversations with sex workers at the clinic, every time I asked why they do what they do, they answered, "Money." However, because money is not an end unto itself, I continued to probe for more information. When I asked about other kinds of jobs they had had, other ways of making money, and the reasons they didn't rely on other forms of employment as their primary source of income, I was able to readily ascertain the local economic picture.

At least 14 percent identified employment difficulties, such as unemployment or insufficient wage, as the primary reason for engaging in sex work. An additional 21 percent were unable to provide for their families, and 6 percent were living on the streets. Combined, at least 31 percent, and perhaps as many as 58 percent, if one includes unspecified economic need, were unable to make ends meet without engaging in sex work. An additional 13 percent, or a total of 44–71 percent, used sex work to obtain education, transportation, a permanent home, or a needed operation for a family member.

Many Tijuana residents are simply unable to make ends meet or to attain their personal goals without resorting to sex work. For those who are poor, sex work means taking personal responsibility for one's livelihood. Unable to sustain themselves through waitressing or factory employment, Modesta and Evonne realized that they could enter prostitution with no prior experience and quickly meet their needs:

> I was working. I was a waitress and I earned very little. I could not cover my expenses. I got off work very late and I started searching in the newspaper. I saw that they needed masseuses and you did not need experience and that they guaranteed $2500 pesos (about $280 U.S.) a week minimum. And with

my need and seeing the money, well: Let's go! And yes, that is how I got started. (Modesta, twenty-one, female sex worker)

Because of the economic situation. They laid off personnel at the assembly plant. And I have to support my little girl and pay for a sitter. (Evonne, nineteen, female sex worker)

Others realize that men are willing to be generous with their sexual partners and thus don't initially start out looking for a "career" per se but take advantage of offers when they can:

I went out with a guy I liked as friends. Once we got to talking, I had sex with him. I did not take precautions and he gave me $200 dollars. Back in my hometown. And I thought it was a lot of money. He knew me, that I was clean. I was not a whore and I had been married before. Now I am with my second husband but I have been with a lot of boys without using a condom and who knows if they may have an infection. I worked in a bar in my town. In Tijuana as a waitress I earned $350 pesos a week. (Patricia, twenty-nine, female sex worker)

Young women like Patricia who work more informally are less likely to become socialized into the profession by experienced, health-conscious workers who have more rigid expectations for condom use. They are less likely to work legally and less likely to take precautions that might protect them from potentially abusive clients. Thus, although someone like Patricia may have fewer lifetime partners overall, the quality of her encounters is more likely to be compromised, placing her at greater risk than those who work on a more regular, formalized basis.

Survival

[I have been working] since I was a little girl, because I left my family at fourteen because I was gay. I helped the whores at a bar get dressed and with their clothes. A soldier offered me $100 pesos and I snapped it up. And the older girls started to show me how. (Antonia, seventeen, male-to-female transgender sex worker)

If parents refuse to accept their child's sexual orientation or gendered performance, as in the case of Antonia, the child may be forced to leave home at an early age. A circle of fictive kinlike relations may develop among those who are excluded from more conventional forms of family. Acting as one another's support system, older generations may also help those with less experience adapt to their new circumstances. Trading everything from makeup to sex tips, Antonia found an easy affinity with local prostitutes, who, as a result of being stigmatized themselves, may be more tolerant than other local residents. Locating such a network may be crucial in helping young people develop a support system that could reduce risk of rape and violence at the hands of clients, strangers, and police.

Others leave home early as a result of physical, emotional, or sexual abuse. A history of abuse is neither necessary nor sufficient to motivate entry into sex work, but it can be a facilitating factor. As Lupe and Maria point out, sex work may be the only way a young person can escape an abusive or unstable household:

> At the age of eleven I left home because I did not get along with my mother's partner, I left with a circus and in order to have a place to stay and food I had sex with the custodian, who was a clown. I left my house because my stepfather beat me and so did my mother. Each one of them broke one of my teeth and my mother also hurt my eye. There I met my eldest daughter's father (he was a police officer). I lasted six months with him and went to Mazatlán to give birth and I never saw him again. I went back to the circus, and then I continued on my own. (Lupe, twenty-one, female sex worker)

> It was very hard. The first time was in Oaxaca. The place where prostitutes work is called Zaragoza. One afternoon it was raining very hard, I had just left school. And I stopped there while the rain stopped, but my mother went by in the family ice truck. She thought that I was engaging in prostitution and she took me to see four doctors so they could say if I was still a virgin. They all said I was. Because of anger towards my mother, I left home at twelve. I went with an aunt and uncle in Puebla and it was there that I started working at that. (Maria, fifteen, female sex worker)

Some, like Anita and Selina, had experienced conflicts with their regular partner that put them over the edge. In these cases, obviously a need for money precipitates the decision, but the first time with a client occurs in the context of emotional turmoil and conflict that may make the decision easier to bear:

When I decided to go look for a job, I was just leaving the house when my husband yelled at me outside, so that everyone would hear: "I want $500 pesos in the house every week!" and I got so mad, that I thought: "I am going to bring that in . . . and more," but not in a maquiladora. So, since I had not studied, I went to work at a massage parlor. (Anita, twenty-eight, female sex worker)

A client insisted and I gave him a massage but I did not have sex with him. The client kept insisting and once, when I was upset with my husband, I did have sex with the client. Eventually I separated from my husband and I continued here. Because of the great amount of money you make here. (Selina, twenty-two, female sex worker)

The impact of gendered power dynamics within the household and the labor market more generally make sex work (and its potential for economic independence) an attractive option for some women. It can give them a sense of power in their personal relationships, a voice in how the household budget is structured, the opportunity to leave a relationship they aren't happy with, and the opportunity to leave an employer who treats them poorly or doesn't pay well. Sex work is an escape strategy that allows women to work around the system when it's not working in their best interests; in this sense, it is a sensible, realistic strategy, given a poor range of options for positive social change.

Single Motherhood and Partner Abandonment

Many sex workers are women with children. In a country that lacks a welfare system, subsidized day care, shelters, food programs, and other public services, the sudden loss of male economic contribution to the household can require a more flexible and profitable way of earning money:

I had just separated from a partner. I had debts. And a nighttime schedule was more agreeable because during the daytime I took care of my three children. I met the owner of a massage parlor and he offered me work. (Rosario, thirty-one, female sex worker)

It was about a year and a half ago. I separated from my little boy's father and went to work as a seamstress but I earned very little. My little boy's father did not give me money and since I was not earning enough, I decided to search and in the newspaper they were looking for masseuses with or without experience, to earn $500 dollars a week. I went to the massage parlor, they told me what it was about and I stayed. (Thalia, twenty-four, female sex worker)

Thirty percent of the female sex workers I interviewed were single mothers who found it impossible to care for themselves and their children on a normal wage and had no other resources to compensate for the gap between the cost of living and the prevalent wage:

> Since about two months ago, economic needs forced me to take this type of job, the reason being that another job did not satisfy my needs and it was very difficult for me, as a single mother, to help my little girl and part of my family, to come out ahead. (Inez, twenty-six, female sex worker)

> The need. We did not have anything to eat in the house. I became desperate. I went looking for work at a massage parlor. I did not know if they had jobs available but I went anyway. (Silvia, nineteen, female sex worker)

Some traveled great distances in order to work in Tijuana:

> I have two children and what I earned back in Sinaloa was not enough to support them. I came over here [to the massage parlor] and I started to earn more money and I stayed. (Flaca, twenty-one, female sex worker)

These narratives make clear that sex workers have been unable to attain the conventional, or at least idealized, situation where a husband is the primary breadwinner and the wife stays at home to take care of the family.[5] Many are unskilled workers who have been abandoned by their partners and have nowhere to turn to provide for their children:

> A boy fooled me with lies, later I got married and six years after my husband left me I came here to earn a living. Hunger made me come here, my husband was not sending anything and I went with two gentlemen, one gave me $50 pesos and another $100, and I ran to feed my three children. I came here to get something to eat. (Dora, twenty-nine, female sex worker)

> [I started] because of a need to generate greater income. My husband left me and my previous job [in a maquiladora] did not pay me enough [$600

pesos per week] for the rent and for my little girl. Through the newspaper I found out about the job at a massage parlor. (Cecilia, twenty-four, female sex worker)

I had been abandoned. I had no partner and I had to support my two babies and my mother also. It seemed to me the best and fastest way for them to live. (Cierra, twenty-eight, female sex worker)

As single mothers, these women must become the primary provider for the household. Some try to make informal relationships with boyfriends, sometimes more than one at a time, in order to obtain money or gifts used to provide for their families:

After the separation from my husband. I had boyfriends and I always wanted them to help me because of my son, but they were just fooling me. So I decided to work a sure thing, as a masseuse. The owner of the pool hall has a massage parlor and he gave me the information. (Pasha, twenty-one, female sex worker)

Others are mothers who may not technically be single but lack the necessary support from their partners and children's fathers:

This is not what I wanted but my husband is not very responsible and I have three children of his and the house where I was living has been sold and I need to get out. (Eva, thirty-two, female sex worker)

My husband was not working and my mother-in-law was supporting us and I had to support my little girl, so I went in as a masseuse. (Manuela, nineteen, female sex worker)

When I became pregnant with my boy eight years ago, I worked for four months before he was born. It was at a restaurant where you went out with the clients in Tijuana. I worked in a massage parlor for a few months three years ago. I work for three months and then I did not work for a year. [I'm waiting until] my husband's [economic] situation gets better. My husband does not know that I work at this. He is 75 years old. (Liliana, thirty, female sex worker)

I had a problem with my husband. We needed money. Along Revolución Avenue I got in a car for money. (Beatriz, nineteen, female sex worker)

[I started because of] a debt on a lot I owned, a lot that I lost because of my partner's irresponsibility. He made all the payments for the house and the boy. He stopped giving me money for expenses. . . . Right now I continue here because I have not seen the response from my husband about supporting me. (Kristina, twenty-five, female sex worker)

Economic Dependence on Men

Women's dependence on men to make ends meet is a product of gender stratification present in Tijuana and in Mexico and Latin America more generally. Females are less likely than men to finish school, having to drop out to meet domestic responsibilities at an early age or because they are viewed as being less worthy of investment by parents, who will invest in the child most likely to succeed and take care of them in their old age (usually male). Occupational opportunities are also highly stratified, either because females lack the necessary skills and education to access certain jobs or because certain jobs (service positions, piecing work, clerical work, etc.) are seen as women's work, and others (professional and managerial work, engineering, civil service) as men's work. Thus, when sex workers say that they started working in the sex trade because of their partner's abandonment or irresponsibility, it is dependence on the male breadwinner that makes abandonment or irresponsibility a significant economic obstacle. In addition, abandonment by a partner, when looked at more closely, can also be seen as a reflection of an unstable economy, high unemployment rates, and the inability of men to find the kind of work that allows them to fulfill the family role (i.e., breadwinner) they aspire to. Policies that make women less dependent upon men to make ends meet or that provide a social safety net for abandoned single mothers would tend to decrease the size of the sex worker labor pool.

Drug Use and Addiction

Because of Tijuana's location along one of the largest international drug smuggling routes, the prevalence of cheap street drugs makes drug addiction very common in Tijuana. The national government has given very little in the way of substance abuse treatment, and the municipal tax base is insufficient to support subsidized treatment. There is only one government-funded rehabilitation center, and it has only a handful of beds. Some small religious-based organizations exist, but they are poorly funded and poorly run. Those who access these services may sleep on the floor with other addicts with nothing but a small blanket and a set of clothes as a pillow. The homes, which can provide very little supervision or counseling, are often in the worst areas of the city, areas where drug use is endemic and temptations are strong. Often, addicts leave one drug-using peer network only to find another in their new neighborhood.

Drug addiction definitely is a factor in the reasons potential sex workers get started in the business:

> Because of need, hunger. First it was for food, then money, later purely for drugs. More for drugs than money. I was seven years old when I started. I slept outside of churches, drunks would arrive to sleep there, first they sought me out and later I sought them out. In cities where there was no gay cruising, I started it, in Oxnard [California], and in Guadalajara. I told them this was how you made easy money. I did not steal. I told them: "Give pleasure and charge for it." (Domíngo, nineteen, male sex worker)

> I started to work [in the sex business] for the need of drugs—because I used drugs before. I started so I could feed my habit, have a small room and eat, at times not even eat. Now I do not spend anything on my habit, I use the money for the hotel and for my baby that is on its way. (Angélica, twenty-three, female sex worker)

> I needed money to pay a debt of 7,000 dollars because I was in jail and that was [the amount] for the bond. A girlfriend told me about the work at a massage parlor, she worked in a massage parlor too. (Irma, twenty-four, female sex worker)

> I danced and sold drugs at a bar, and I knew the Zone [the Zona Norte] because I also had work with *pollos* [literally chickens, people trying to cross the border] here. A year ago they deported me after being in jail on drug charges and because I had debts in San Diego I started in prostitution on Callejón Coahuila. (Graciela, twenty-eight, female sex worker)

> Here in Tijuana, it is the way that you get easy money because I was hooked on crystal. (Gabriel, twenty-two, male sex worker)

> A year ago they put my partner in jail. I was too hooked and well, it was the easiest thing. (Miranda, thirty-one, female sex worker)

> I had just arrived in Tijuana and I already liked men as well as women. I had an economic problem [paying for rent] and I did not have a job. There

were two gays where I lived, I made friends with them and one offered me
money and since I had the damn noose around my neck [addiction], I did it.
(Marín, twenty-two, male sex worker)

Drug addiction not only motivates entry into sex work, it plays a factor in
keeping a sex worker in the business.

Supporting a Lifestyle

For some sex workers, earning money through sex work allows access to a
glamorous consumer-oriented lifestyle, while others simply enjoy making
what they see as easy money:

> I stayed because you earn a lot, and I like living well and dressing well. I
> liked the idea and I started. Not out of necessity or anything. (Ramón,
> twenty-two, male sex worker)

Going out to bars, fancy restaurants, traveling, and having the latest clothes,
makeup, jewelry, and accessories are associated with middle- and upper-class
lifestyles. Attaining this lifestyle is both symbolic, in terms of being able to
acquire a certain level of social status, and pleasurable, in terms of enhanced
leisure time, aesthetics, and being able to indulge in sensory pleasures. In
addition, because gay community life revolves around parties, bars, and dance
clubs, there is an additional incentive for gay-identified male and transgender
workers to acquire a disposable income.

Most of the sex workers who participated in my study made more than
enough money to make ends meet. This was especially true of women working in massage parlors and the most popular brothel/nightclubs like Adelitas
Bar or Chicago Club, which are heavily oriented toward sex tourists from
the United States and Asia and well-to-do Mexican businessmen. In fact,
more than 17 percent occasionally had sex with their customers in exchange
for luxury goods rather than money, a higher percentage than those who had
sex in exchange for shelter (3 percent) or food (10 percent). In Mexico, where
the majority of the populace is working class or underclass with no disposable
income, access to a consumer-oriented lifestyle is largely unaffordable. Thus,
for a few, sex work is not an act of desperation, but a kind of work they find
enjoyable and easy:

> I saw the possibility of earning a lot of money in very little time, and besides,
> it satisfies me. (Serina, nineteen, male-to-female transgender sex worker)

Having fun with friends and meeting a potential mate (especially one who is economically stable) can be a costly endeavor. For some sex workers, becoming involved in sex work is an extension of their everyday social activities with their peers or an extension of their previous sexual relations with other men. Sex workers may learn about the work through their friends (as discussed earlier), but in addition socialization with friends may overlap with sex work activities. This pattern emerged primarily with male and transgender sex workers like Jesús, Simón, and Serina:

> I already felt attracted to men and I went [to a gay disco]. A person I met there invited me to go to his house. And "it happened" in his house. I was ashamed to ask him for money and he gave me what he wanted. I do not remember how much it was. (Jesús, twenty-one, male sex worker)

> I came to Tijuana looking for a hometown friend, but he had already died from AIDS. Since I did not have a place to live, around that time I met a gay professional man and he rented a room in a hotel for me and he stayed too. Later he got me a job out of town. I was away two months and then I went back home. About a year later I returned married but I was already connected to the gay life. (Simon, twenty-three, male sex worker)

> First I was a transvestite. I impersonated artists. I wanted to have friends the same as myself. Near my house I saw a drag queen. I followed her home and knocked at the door, I made friends with her. I started to talk and told her I wanted to get dressed up and put on makeup. Then she took me to the disco and they did not let me in because I was underage (in Guadalajara). The doorman cruised me and I took the opportunity to get in, and later I was able to get in. They hid me when the regulations inspectors arrived. I did impersonations but later I saw that you could earn more money offstage and so I started. (Serina, nineteen, male-to-female transgender sex worker)

This kind of attitude was not common among female sex workers, perhaps for both social and economic reasons. Female sex workers appear to make more rigid distinctions between their home and work life. The greater cultural emphasis on sexual respectability for women may be one reason for this; the fact that they have a higher prevalence of marriage and family may be another. Both the reasons for entering sex work and the way in which one enters appear to be highly gendered. This is not to say that there are no similarities among male, female, and transgender sex workers—but there are some important differences that need to be acknowledged if one hopes to understand the context of their work.

Sexual Entrepreneurship

In the end, sex work is likely popular because of its entrepreneurial nature. Sex workers own their own means of production. In a regulated sex industry like that of Tijuana, legal workers work as independent contractors. They have the opportunity to set their own hours and fees and are not bound by any contracts. They have rights and guarantees afforded to them by the government, including consistent, high-quality health care and the right to work without harassment by the police. They tend to make a better income than people in any other form of work. If successful, they are able to build their first house, send their siblings and children to high school and college, purchase a vehicle, and even invest in real estate.

The goals of sex workers in Tijuana are unattainable elsewhere in Mexico. The lack of a strong municipal tax base throughout Mexico makes even a high school education a difficult proposition. Thus, for sex workers in Tijuana, the aspiration might be to merely complete high school, which requires money for books and uniforms. Given the obvious shortfall of housing discussed in chapter 2, many of the sex workers I met were saving to buy a home for themselves or their parents. They might already have shelter, living in a rented home, but they want the kind of status that comes from owning their own home.[6] Often, they were saving to build that home in their hometown, leaving Tijuana once they accomplished that goal.

The paradox of using stigmatized work to realize social advancement is apparent. However, when people chose sex work not out of desperation but as a calculated maneuver to fulfill economic ambitions, the sense of desperation that can emerge as a result of engaging in this kind of work is lessened. The sense of personal control is much stronger.

Some of the first investments made by those in a stronger financial situation are body modifications, such as remedial dentistry, breast implants, hormone injections, genital surgery (sex change), hair weaves, manicures, etc. Diet and exercise are also common fixations, requiring the purchase of gym membership, personal trainers, high nutrient/low-calorie foods, herbs, creams, teas, and pills. These enable higher earnings, but they are also very important to enhancing self-esteem because they allow conformance to cultural aesthetics.

Sex workers are far from indifferent to the never-ending cycle of consumerist desire. In discussing consumerism, McCracken (1990) notes that culture and consumption have an unprecedented relationship in the modern world. . . . The consumer goods on which the consumer lavishes time, attention, and income are charged with cultural meaning. . . . Consumers use this meaning to . . . express cultural categories and principles, cultivate ideals, create and sustain lifestyles, construct notions of the self, and create (and survive) social change. (xi)

Although sex workers are considered deviant, in reality they have ambitions similar to those entertained by people in other kinds of work.[7] The analysis of historical consumer trends, the effect of globalization in shaping consumer desires, and the role of mass media in constructing those images, while outside the scope of my research, are relevant considerations in understanding the advantages of sex work over other kinds of work. Clearly, some sex workers work from a consumer-oriented perspective rather than out of desperation.[8] Though customers frame the ambition among sex workers as greed, research by anthropologists, sociologists, activists, and sex-positive feminists paints a different picture. Accounts vary from academic activism[9] to full-length autobiographical accounts by sex workers who want to communicate the advantages they have gained through their profession.[10]

Conclusions

Currently in Tijuana neither law nor policy makes an effort to differentiate between workers, and there are no specialized programs serving the needs of this highly diverse workforce. Because of the connections among the circumstances surrounding one's entrance into the commercial sex industry, one's experiences on the job, and one's exposures to and ability to avoid occupational risks, this diversity needs to be acknowledged and incorporated into tailored programs that empower sex workers to make the best of their personal circumstances.

CHAPTER FOUR

Commercial Sex and the Social Landscape

*My attention is caught by a doorman sitting on a stool in front of a local
nightclub. It's a sunny day, warm, dry, but not unbearable. Like San Diego,
except for the strong smell of beer and food wafting down the thoroughfare. A
heavy blue velvet curtain covers the entryway—and the doorman beckons me
and my two male friends into the club. "Free drinks for the ladies," he says, and
I am eager to peer inside but my friends are hesitant. The lurid reputation of
the Tijuana sex scene encourages me to talk them into going inside; that same
reputation makes them reluctant to enter, at least in female company. Will the
reality of these settings resemble the myths? Finally, they agree to enter. Inside, it's
dark and musty, only a few patrons in this bar, unlike many of the others we've
visited. Recognizing the name of this club, I know that it's likely that some of
its employees will be different from what they appear to be at first glance—this
club is infamous for its transgender workers. We sit down, and get our drinks.
I light a cigarette, and one of the employees sits down next to my friend, who I
have strategically placed on the outside of the booth. She doesn't speak very much
English, but the journey of her hand on his thigh makes it clear that he is being
solicited. He waves her away, only to have four more workers sit next to him over
the next hour. One by one, each of the workers try to encourage him to take her to
a hotel, only to leave discouraged. If I were a man, at least this would give me a
point of entry to start chatting them up, but they aren't interested in talking with
me, and probably more than uncomfortable by my presence at the table. It's going
to be difficult to establish rapport in these settings. But I will do what I can to
spend time in every club on this street, and hope that eventually someone will take
an interest in my project.*

FIELD NOTES, MAY 1, 1999.

My first exposure to the commercial sex industry in Tijuana happened on Avenida Revolución. A busy avenue attracting mostly U.S. tourists, this street has a number of strip clubs and bars that resemble those found in the United States. The visible presence of sexual commerce in this area normalizes the purchase of sex as just another commodity. I learned from talking informally with a variety of U.S. sex tourists that, like the blankets, pottery, Coronas, and food sold on La Revolución, the sexual experience provided in these areas is seen as quintessentially Mexican. Many customers view gendered performances by *mexicana* sex workers as a natural characteristic based on cultural difference rather than a product of female economic dependence and strategic marketing. In their search for what they see as a more "traditional" woman, many engage in longer-term partnerships with sex workers over the border.

Customers of the Tijuana sex industry, both U.S.-based and otherwise, encompass a wide diversity of class, ethnic, occupational, and migratory backgrounds as well as sexual preferences. Mexican nationals, including seasonal migrant workers, migrants seeking permanent residence either in Tijuana or across its border in the United States, Mexican tourists or traveling business professionals, and permanent Tijuana residents comprise the most significant portions of the population of customers. Non-Mexican nationals, including U.S. nationals crossing into Tijuana for leisurely tourist pursuits, Asian businessmen associated with the *maquiladora* industry, and a smaller segment of Asians seeking entry into the United States comprise other significant portions of this population. As particular segments of the industry cater to this very diverse clientele, it is difficult to characterize the industry as a whole without risk of overgeneralization. There is, however, at least one element of the industry that touches all who work in it: the impact of laws related to prostitution and the practices surrounding the enforcement of those laws.

Laws related to prostitution are an integral part of the Tijuana social landscape. These laws, and the policies and practices surrounding them, result from the social negotiation of what constitutes moral or criminal action (or both) as it relates to sex. As the economic and political environment shifts, so too does the level of interest in sexual and moral issues. Within this rapidly urbanizing metropolitan area, fears about social chaos and moral decline have intensified. The enforcement of existing laws related to prostitution has fluctuated in response to popular demands, media stories, and changing municipal leadership. Fluctuating enforcement is spurred on by the changing definition of what constitutes prostitution, what kinds of prostitution or groups of prostitutes are seen as dangerous, and what the appropriate response is to the growing numbers of prostitutes (especially those under the age of eighteen).

There is no consensus on what kinds of prostitution (if any) should be tolerated; nor is there consensus on the impact of legal regulations related to prostitution. The role of scientific evidence is not clear, partly because there is a paucity of research in this area and partly because the evidence that does exist from research studies in other cities is rarely disseminated to key decision makers. A variety of constituents have a vested interest in prostitution reform. Local residents, the health care sector, and the tourism sector are all potentially impacted by legal reforms and fluctuating enforcement. Obviously, sex workers and their customers also are directly affected by these issues. If the future of reform is anything like past changes, it is not likely that the latter will have much of a voice in how prostitution will be dealt with at the city level.

As my findings will demonstrate, there are political, legal, and bodily consequences to the regulation and policing of particular prostitutes' bodies. The everyday experience of sex workers in Tijuana includes a variety of occupational hazards, many of which are exacerbated by the practice of regulation and policing. Some groups of sex workers benefit from legal regulations; others experience greatly increased risks to their personal safety. The social inequalities found within the sex work hierarchy of sex workers reflect and reinforce those found in the city more generally. Access to safe work venues is limited by both social and legal status, both of which have synergistic effects with one another.

The Police

While I was living in Tijuana, border police would sit on the U.S. side of the border only five blocks from my apartment. Mexican police, who often carry assault rifles and other powerful guns, were even more prevalent, roaming the beaches in front of my building, driving up and down the streets throughout my neighborhood and the downtown area where I worked. The police were rough, suspicious, and intimidating—violence, corruption, and extortion run rampant in today's headlines. A common phrase was repeated to me no matter where I visited in Mexico: "The only thing you have to fear here is the police." Having come from a relatively sheltered middle-class area in the United States, I found this to be an astonishing cultural difference, although it might match the sentiments of residents in poor urban areas like South Central Los Angeles. It became apparent that every move I made outside my house was subject to surveillance. I became very interested in how this environment shaped the experiences of the sex workers I included in my study.

Through my experiences in Tijuana, I discovered that legal policy surrounding sex work is enormously important in shaping occupational risks in the industry. As the politics of sex work vary from neighborhood to neighborhood, city to city, county to county, and country to country, the particular legal frameworks which those politics have helped shape also vary. There are three dominant types of legal frameworks found throughout the world, none of which has succeeded in eradicating sex work, and all of which shape the daily occupational risks that sex workers face. These three frameworks are

- Criminalization through prohibition—All sex work is illegal, and all sex workers can be prosecuted under the law (though punishments vary from jurisdiction to jurisdiction);
- Decriminalization—The police take a "hands off" approach, seeking neither to regulate nor criminalize sex work; and
- Legalization through regulation—Sex work is legal, usually within defined boundaries through zoning laws or through registration; sex work outside of this regulated system is usually treated as a criminal offence.

The official policy on sex work in Tijuana is one of legal regulation. Sex work is regulated through worker registration, including health cards and mandatory screenings for sexually transmitted infections (STIs); site licensing, with regular inspections for illegal sex workers; and *zonas de tolerancia*. However, not all sex workers or establishments work within this formal system. In fact, because many sex workers do not register with the city clinic in order to obtain health cards and screenings, sex work often takes place outside of this system. Those who work illegally are treated as criminals and are subject to prosecution that can bring fines and jail time. They sometimes face extortion, police harassment, and assault, including rape. Like the state of Nevada in the United States, this system can be characterized as a bifurcated industry with both a formal and legal sector and an informal and illegal sector. However, in contrast to Nevada, the formal and informal sectors overlap spatially and are tightly integrated with the mainstream economy.[1]

It is the formal and legalized sector that tends to dominate discussion of the Tijuana sex industry, both in the media and among public health and social science researchers. The regulatory system, while it can be improved in a variety of ways, acts as a form of harm reduction for sex workers in the formal sector and is considered a relatively successful model in maintaining low rates of STIs. Ironically, it is not so much the mandated monthly health screenings that affect workers' overall occupational risk. Rather, it is their legal status, which provides a form of social capital and a set of protections, that has a positive impact on occupational health and safety. This variable should be seen, then, as more of a social variable than a clinical or biomedical one. Among other things, registration encourages professionalization and protective health behaviors, encourages police cooperation and protection, and discourages police and client violence, all of which enhance a sex worker's ability to avoid occupational hazards, including STIs.

As I will demonstrate in the following chapters, gender, age, sexual orientation, and documentation status systematically discourage and sometimes exclude registration of particular sex workers and their entry into the formal sector. The experiences of legal workers, who often work in the informal sector, are quite different, yet their experiences are not represented in official portrayals of the "success" of the formal sector. Because illegal workers appear to be more vulnerable, both in terms of their social, economic, and health status prior to sex work and in terms of the increased risk due to their illegal status, I specifically sought out illegal workers in order to capture how work experiences in the formal and informal sector differed.

Social Hierarchy of Work Venues

Sexual commerce in Tijuana is racialized, heteronormative, and classed. That is, at the top of the hierarchy are women of European appearance, who service a male heterosexual clientele. Those at the top of the hierarchy tend to have greater economic resources to begin with or are able to escape at least the appearance of poverty by making investments in their physical appearance and language skills. The social organization of the sex industry is reflected and reinforced through the hierarchy of work venues in the city. Relationships of power and an understanding of what is good, clean, or at least safe commercial sex are defined through city regulations that make some work venues legal and others illegal. Legal work venues are safer than those that are illegal, they have better working conditions, and they allow those who work on the premises to make more money per customer. The social stigma attached to these work settings is also lessened, workers are considered cleaner, safer, and more professional, and there is a strong emphasis on creating a friendly, pleasant atmosphere for upscale clients.

By delineating what kinds of sex work are deemed criminal and what kinds of sex workers are subject to fines and imprisonment, sex work regulations reinforce ideas about who is a legitimate citizen worthy of public services and police protection. Those who work outside of the legal system are denied legitimacy and work as criminals: subject to a full range of additional occupational hazards because of their illegal status. These regulations acknowledge and sanction only those at the very top of the social hierarchy within the sex industry, further marginalizing those at the bottom and making social mobility more difficult and more dangerous.

In the formal sector, sexual commerce between female sex workers and male customers is highly institutionalized and regulated in a way that attracts tourists without offending the moral decency of local residents. Strict zoning laws and licensing procedures permit the city to enjoy the benefits of the industry without appearing to be irresponsible and exploitative. Sexual commerce between men and women is a highly integrated and naturalized part of the recreational landscape of the downtown area.

Upscale Establishments

Sexy but "tasteful" images on billboards, flyers, and commercial establishments reinforce the normalcy of upscale sexual commerce as part of Tijuana's legitimate economy and service industry. The images provided are not too explicit but still provocative and illustrate well-dressed, youthful, model-like Latinas with strong European ancestry and come-hither looks. Advertisements for topless massage, gentlemen's clubs, and escort services, all of which cater to a more middle-class professional clientele from both Mexico and the United States, are the most frequently seen by passersby in the border zone. Such advertisements also dominate the entertainment sections of both local newspapers. The more ambiguous nature of advertised services is met with less resistance in a city attempting to promote its "family" tourist base and renew its image.

Within these establishments, a customer will find an activity similar to that in establishments in the United States: strip dancing and featured dancers—something not too foreign but foreign enough to be enticing. Workers must meet customers' expectations in order to make money. In upscale establishments, this means that the worker must be able to conform to the glamorous imagery seen in advertisements. This imagery is highly classed and racialized, and the workers who are able to conform to these expectations tend to be educated and worldly—they are expected to converse easily with strangers, sometimes in English, to laugh at the customer's jokes, and to cater to his fantasies. Acting and social skills help them successfully paint an extended portrait of an infatuated lover or an innocent girl. Sex worker participants from this sector of the industry reported spending more time with clients, developing a regular clientele base, and refining their professional skills. Many saw themselves as part therapist, stating that many customers wanted intimacy or conversation that were lacking in their lives. Several workers spent a large portion of their income on beauty enhancements, such as plastic surgery, including breast implants and nose jobs, braces, makeup, gym memberships, and special foods and snacks, creams, and teas, and on social enhancements, such as language classes, travel, and dance. For the most part, they were more body conscious and fashion conscious than sex workers in other settings, and they saw their investments as directly related to their future earning potential. All were adamant about condom use and personal hygiene as part of their professional standards. Many saw this as the primary distinction between their kind of work venues and those of the lower class. While they saw themselves as clean and healthy, they spoke about women in other sectors as unprofessional, dirty, and diseased.

Several had specific goals connected with their income: they wanted to open their own business (sometimes their own massage parlor), jewelry store, or an Internet café. A few had plans to purchase land to build rental properties. Many of those who worked to put themselves through school were taking classes to prepare them for law school or college, or they were hoping to get married and raise a family. Although they had less turnover in customers, they were able to make from eighty to two hundred dollars per session, earning an average of two thousand dollars a month. The most successful sex workers could earn up to five thousand dollars a month during the summer tourist season, but most workers who made more than a few thousand a month only worked intermittently. Workers at this level often complained that they weren't able to save their money or invest their money properly and so continued to work in spite of having made much more than their initial goal.

Working- and Middle-Class Establishments

In reality, the upscale establishments are the exception to the rule—the majority of sex work establishments cater to working-class and middle-class patrons of Mexican origin. The sex workers in these establishments are more representative of the average *mexicana*—a bit shorter, a bit darker, and usually somewhat older than the women found in the tonier clubs. Dress and demeanor are more conservative, there are less likely to be shows with featured dancers, and the dancers are more likely to engage in dancing with the customers. The population boom along the border ensures that the work in these establishments is still lucrative; many of the women in these clubs make an average of forty to eighty dollars per transaction, or about a thousand to twenty-five hundred dollars a month.

Many of these workers lived permanently in Tijuana and were saving to buy a local business, build a house, buy a car, put themselves through school, care for children, or pay off debts. Clothing stores, little boutiques, and beauty parlors were the most sought-after businesses. Some of the workers were waiting for their partners to get out of a rehabilitation center or jail, others were waiting for passports or *polleros* to help them cross into the United States so that they could be with family members or pursue a more conventional life. Several explained that they were saving so that they could eventually settle down and spend more time with their families at home. Many were hoping for another job to come along or were training to work in the beauty industry or the computer industry. Most were high school graduates or at least had received some high school education, and they socialized with customers who more or less reflected their own social and economic backgrounds.

On the Street

A large majority of sex workers don't work in these establishments at all, but on the street and in parks and plazas as well as more informally through neighborhood bars, restaurants, cafes, parties, or out of their homes. These workers are a highly diverse cross-section of people, reflecting the social diversity found in the city itself. The majority are newcomers to Tijuana, primarily migrants from southern areas of Mexico, *indígenas* from the Yucatán or the Guatemalan Highlands, and immigrants from Central America. Many are undocumented or underage and are forced to work illegally. Such workers differ in physical and social characteristics, making it difficult for them to conform to the expectations of customers in upscale establishments. Most of them also explained that they were uncomfortable working in a nightclub scene because it wasn't familiar to them, they didn't like the ambience of smoke, alcohol, and drugs, and they didn't like socializing or partying with their customers. They emphasized that they were working simply to make money, they wanted the transactions over with as quickly as possible, and they were not in Tijuana to have fun.

These workers were more likely than others to have concrete, short-term goals, such as saving to build a family home or buy a family business, like a little grocery or restaurant, back in their sending community. Most planned to return permanently someday, and many worked in Tijuana only during the busy season. Several were just trying to survive in a country with few other viable options. The majority had received a little elementary schooling but had never attended high school. Some were working to get their elementary diploma so that they could continue their studies. They made about twenty dollars per customer transaction and spent an average of fifteen minutes in the room with their customers. Many chose to stay dressed during the exchange; even though undressing usually brought them extra money, it made them feel uncomfortably vulnerable. These workers generally made from five hundred to a thousand dollars per month, depending on how often they worked.

Conclusion

The contours of the sex industry are gendered, racialized, and classed. The setting is largely heteronormative, but alternate gender and sexual relations are given social space. The social landscape, which is fraught with inequalities, largely determines working conditions and therefore the likelihood of exposure to occupational health risks. While labor and demand for a sex industry are created by macrolevel economic forces like rural to urban migration and social inequality, the contours of the industry are shaped by forces which are more social and cultural in nature. Entry into sex work should be seen in this context.

CHAPTER FIVE

Legal Status and Policing

In Tijuana, fear of sex workers as vectors of sexually transmitted infection (STI) has led to calls for their increased regulation via registration, mandatory testing, and criminal penalties. Though this system is intrusive, it does benefit those who work legally in that their legal status allows them access to the safest and most profitable venues, affords protection from police, and facilitates the professionalization process. The system may also work to socialize those new to the industry, by emphasizing the importance of condom use and regular screening and treatment for STIs. Those who work outside of the system, however, face added risk as a result of their illegal status. Policing strategies have a definitive impact on occupational risk for violence, mental health problems, and STIs, including HIV/AIDS. In this chapter, I compare the differing risks faced by legal and illegal workers and discuss how their distinct legal status and relationship with the police mitigate or, in the case of illegal workers, increase occupational risks.

In comparing health outcomes of workers according to their legal status, I will focus on female workers. I do this for two reasons. First, legal status itself is highly gendered. That is, only female workers are targeted by health inspectors in charge of health card surveillance. As a result, only females and a small number of male-to-female transgender workers are registered in the clinic. Second, although gender is one of the primary factors shaping occupational experiences and exposure to occupational risks, there are a number of statistically significant differences in working conditions and health outcomes based on legal status alone. Although I will include a few of the personal narratives of all participants (regardless of gender), my statistics are limited to female workers. Thus, for the purposes of this discussion I eliminated male sex workers (all of whom are illegal) and transgender sex workers (some of whom are legal but can't be compared with one another statistically because of the small sample size) and focus only on the statistical differences between female workers working either legally or illegally. In the next chapter, I will outline the differences between female, male, and transgender sex workers as a result of gender status and sexual orientation.

Structural Violence

The exclusion of particular sectors of the workforce, especially those that are the most vulnerable, is a form of structural violence that makes the legalization and regulation framework less than ideal. Structural violence, as defined by Anglin (1998),

> takes such forms as the expropriation of vital economic and non-material re-sources and the operation of systems of social stratification or categorization that subvert people's chances for survival . . . [and] can be understood as the imposition of categories of difference that legitimate hierarchy and inequality . . . [and] deny them the opportunity for emotional and physical well-being, or expose them to assault or rape, or subject them to hazards that can cause sickness and death.

The category of structural violence includes, among other things, slavery, racism, poverty, and social inequality, exclusion and domination, unemployment, and forced migration as well as sets of social norms or government policies that have an adverse impact on quality of life (Anglin 1998; Farmer 2004; Singer 1998; Singer et al. 1992). Included in the category of structural violence are policies such as criminalization and incarceration, policies which on the surface are seen as a commonsense way to stabilize the social order but are experienced as a form of social injustice that does little to address prevention issues and safety.

The idea of structural violence can seem to be a somewhat fuzzy concept if not directly connected to concrete examples (Wacquant 2004). But this framework is crucial in relation to occupational health and safety, as it allows one to move beyond the victim/perpetrator dichotomy at the level of the individual and into those social settings that encourage, produce, or otherwise enable violence of the more physical kind. Because risk for workplace violence is such a significant issue among sex workers, it is critical that one develop a holistic understanding of the social determinants of their occupational health.

Formal and Informal Sectors

In Tijuana, the work itself consists of a wide variety of sexual activities, work sites, and methods of solicitation, including street work, hustling, stripping, table dancing, *fichera* dancing (dancing with customers for tips), massage parlors, escort/call services, private brothels—each of which includes differing expectations for compensation, negotiation, sexual practices, and condom use and faces varying levels of surveillance by health inspectors and police. The formal sector includes primarily legal workers, but illegal workers also work in some venues with the consent of management (but not of health inspectors).

Some work sites are visited more frequently by health inspectors than others, but inspectors have a very defined and predictable set of establishments to visit, and they know many of the workers by name. The inspectors look for those who have let their card lapse or who should not be working because they are being treated for an STI. When a team of inspectors visits a site, they first check the workers' health cards, which are held by the manager, and then check to see if anyone without a current health card is working in the establishment. I have seen workers hide in the bathroom or under tables or go out the back in order to avoid being detected by inspectors. If someone is caught working illegally, they are written up and forced to leave work. Subsequent incidents entail steadily increasing fines and potential jail time if the worker is unable to pay the fine. Owners may also be fined based on repeat occurrences; they may eventually also lose their license. Owners never face jail time, making the employment of illegal workers fairly profitable for them in terms of increased sales.

Health inspection is specific to geography and venue as well as highly gendered. Female and transgender sex workers are more likely to be targeted than male sex workers, primarily because of the more clandestine nature of commercial and noncommercial sex between men. Health inspectors tend to visit only the most visible commercial sites, usually those in clear sight of tourists in the Zona Norte, the main red light district. *Fichera* and strip bars are the largest commercial establishments and are visited frequently by health inspectors. This district is tightly integrated into the tourist economy and is in close physical proximity to tourist and commercial sex establishments (see the accompanying map of the Zona Norte). In the Zona Norte, inspections focus on sex workers working on or near Coahuila and along Avenida Revolución, both high-traffic areas for tourists, shoppers, and migrant workers. Avenida Revolución, which caters to both male and female tourists from the United States, tends to have massage parlors and strip clubs; not all workers have sex

ZONA NORTE (TOURIST ZONE, COMMERCIAL DISTRICT)

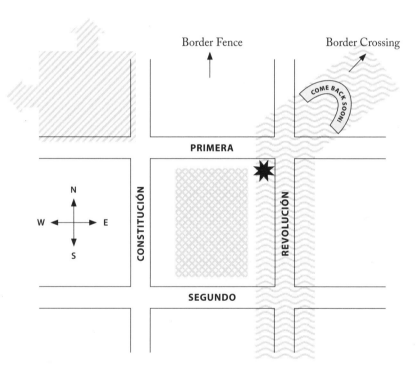

COAHUILA Brothels, Fichera Halls, Strip Clubs, Hotels

AVE. REVOLUCIÓN Tourist Foot Traffic, Curios, Restaurants, Liquor Stores, Dentists, Pharmacies, Bars, Strip Clubs, Nightclubs

PLAZA STA. CECILIA Gay Bars, Bars, Hotels, Vendors, Restaurants, Liquor Stores, Dentists, Pharmacies, Community Events

SECRETARY OF TOURISM

Border Fence

Border Crossing

COME BACK SOON

PRIMERA

N
W ← → E
S

CONSTITUCIÓN

REVOLUCIÓN

SEGUNDO

with customers in these establishments. The strip clubs, located in a ten-block area along Revolución, are less visible than they were a decade ago; some have moved to the side streets of the avenue in order to make the main tourist strip more family friendly. Independent vendors, beggars, and hair stylists work along these edges as well, knowing they will be hassled or fined by police if they hustle for customers on the avenue itself. Most restaurant staff and shop vendors along the avenue speak at least some English, as the majority of their customers are from the United States.

The Coahuila area, encompassing about a four-block area, is not a family-oriented tourist center. It is located only a block or two away from Avenida Revolución, but signs and road blocks direct the flow of tourist foot traffic away from these streets. It is heavily saturated with visible sex work establishments, half-hour motels, doormen, hawkers, vendors, cabbies, and, of course, street workers. Although illegal workers in other neighborhoods might stroll along the sidewalks, these sex workers stand beside one another along the building facades, speaking to potential customers who look interested in a date. The accompanying map illustrates the density of sex establishments and street workers in and around Coahuila. Other tolerance zones, such as the middle-class business areas in La Mesa, are not heavily scrutinized by either health inspectors or police, perhaps because much of it is indoors and removed from the tourist district.

The formal sector provides a profitable enterprise for those directly involved in the trade (workers, staff, management, owners) and those who make their living by exploiting the trade (police, health inspectors, cab drivers, drug dealers, and liquor stores) and a horde of specialized clothing vendors, beauty salons, makeup saleswomen, herbalists, pharmacies, doctors, jewelry stores, and electronics stores—all of whom tailor their wares to meet the special needs of their sex worker clientele and provide an outlet for consumption activities. For example, herbalist vendors are located just off of Coahuila, where they sell diet pills and teas, cellulite cream, herbs, and amulets to prevent or treat STIs, in addition to massage oil, snake oil,[1] and herbal Viagra-like products. Within the informal sector, the popularity of solicitation areas rises and falls according to seasonal climate changes and policing strategies. Illegal workers tend to work in areas that have less police surveillance, such as beaches, parks, restaurants, call services (phone), massage parlors, and streets as well as nightclubs and bars outside the Zona Norte. Relationships with police tend to be hostile, and illegal workers are subjected to fines and jail time as well as police harassment, extortion, violence, and rape.

These sites vary in terms of the visibility of sex work transactions. Parks, beaches, alleys, and side streets (except for the streets near Coahuila), where the majority of the most at-risk sex workers work, are not usually targeted by health inspectors but are subject to surveillance by police.

Although migrant workers and local businessmen actually comprise the largest regular customer base for the majority of the establishments, on weekends and evenings males from the United States cross the border in search of paid sex. Sexual services in the formal sector are more visible and easier to

COAHUILA (ZONA NORTE, ZONA ROJA)

☆   Free-Standing Hotel

⊗   Parking

▲   Brothels, Fichera Dance Halls, Strip Clubs
     (41 in 4 square block area)

▨   Visible Street Hooking

Plaza Sta. Cecilia and
Ave. Revolución

locate and are more likely to be utilized by tourists or those less familiar with the city. The cost of services varies substantially within both sectors but tends to be higher in the formal sector. Customers who seek services in the informal sector may have less money, may be longtime visitors or residents of Tijuana, or may seek services not available in the formal economy. These customers include underage workers, male workers, "rough trade," etc. For those familiar with the city, finding services outside the Zona Norte may be more convenient or less stressful in terms of the ambiguity involved. Customers, who don't have to worry about being prosecuted by the police, may negotiate services with less fear of being caught by their neighbors, friends, or wives.

Legal Workers

I found that legal sex workers were at the very top of the social hierarchy—they have better working conditions and job satisfaction, less fear about the nature of their work, and a higher degree of sophistication and confidence with regard to their speaking skills, appearance, and demeanor. Registration and monthly checkups appear to encourage behaviors that are protective of health as well as provide a barrier against police harassment. Registration increases the sense of legitimacy and community and is correlated with much lower levels of depression and mental stress.

Within the formal system, city health inspectors are responsible for making random visits to bars and streets in *zonas de tolerancia* in order to ensure that each woman has a current health card. In 1999, 302 new sex workers registered with Servicios Médicos Municipales, the city clinic responsible for distributing health cards. The 1,000 women whom the clinic served that year came once a month to receive lab tests for syphilis and cervical cancer. They were also checked for visible signs of gonorrhea, genital warts, herpes, inflammation, and other infections. HIV tests were given every four months, and about half of all the new legal workers were tested on their knowledge, attitude, and practice of the risks and prevention of HIV/AIDS.[2]

After paying an initial registration fee of about sixty-five dollars, sex workers who passed the exam had their health cards stamped with the following month's exam date and were permitted to work in *zonas de tolerancia,* usually the Zona Norte. Mandatory monthly checkups are required in order to keep the health card valid and current. In the case of a positive test or visible symptoms of an STI, sex workers were given antibiotics or other appropriate medications and had to wait a specified period of time for their follow-up exam. If they passed the follow-up exam, their health card was stamped, and

Figures 5.1a, b. Herbal vendor's products in Zona Norte. This vendor sells diet teas, cellulite creams, and herbal Viagra-like supplements along with charms and magical oils for increased profits, love spells, and health protection. Herbal supplements said to treat sexually transmitted infections, including HIV/AIDS, are also available.

they were permitted to return to work. Health cards were confiscated if an HIV test came back positive. In 1999 four cards had been confiscated because of positive HIV/AIDS tests.

After being targeted by health inspectors, women found to be working without health cards were given a written warning and information about how to obtain a card. Women who ignored this warning and were found to be working without a card were fined about twenty dollars. Bribes, including sexual favors, were known to be given to circumvent this system. Additional infractions meant increased fines (or more bribes or sexual favors)—however, the director of the clinic was unaware of any workers who had continued working illegally after the first time they were fined.

Health cards are not given to anyone under eighteen years of age or to non-Mexican nationals or those without official documentation. Photo IDs and birth certificates, which many people in Mexico, especially those from rural areas, don't have, are required by all registering sex workers. Bars must obtain a special license from the city in order to employ sex workers, and although health inspectors have suspended the licenses of a few bars for allowing under-aged workers to work illegally, club owners and customers have never been targeted for criminal prosecution for employing a sex worker who is working illegally. Massage parlors, call services, and private brothels are not licensed to employ sex workers and not targeted by health inspectors. Male staff members are not required to register for health cards. Most work as managers, waiters, bouncers, bartenders, or doormen. A few turn tricks on the side, and many have sexual relations with the female or transgender workers on the prem-ises. Although outside the scope of this book, the role of support staff in the sexual networks of sex workers should be considered in more comprehensive studies.

This book is not a random sample of sex workers, for reasons I explained in the introductory chapter. As such, this study is not evidence that most sex workers are illegal—no official sources I know of give any estimate of the numbers of illegal and legal sex workers. I know only that approximately one thousand sex workers are legally registered in any given year and that this number remained relatively stable over the period 1999–2002. Even with about three hundred newly legal sex workers each year, the average number of those working legally seems to stay the same, with many workers choosing to leave the Tijuana sex industry for work elsewhere. It's also likely that some

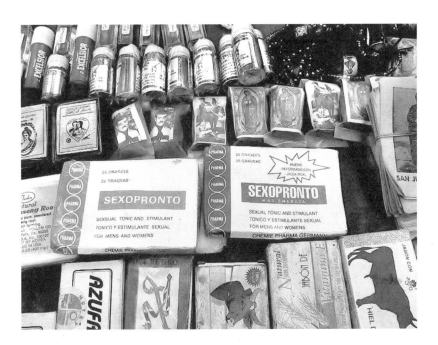

find ways around the registration system, choosing to minimize costs by obtaining medical services only when they deem it necessary. Many sex workers allow their health cards to lapse, either because they are working seasonally or because they are low on cash and don't want to pay for the exam—the clinic does not maintain a tracking system that would indicate how often such lapses occur.

The city clinic is therefore responsible for giving up to twelve thousand exams a year, an average of thirty-three exams each day. Business is heaviest toward the end of each month, when workers must update their cards in order to continue to work legally. There are usually two doctors and one nurse on staff on any given day as well as an unlicensed staff member who acts as an intake reporter and counselor and three receptionists to take questions, handle appointments, and sell condoms for ten cents apiece. The doctors, likely the highest paid of anyone in the clinic, make only ten thousand dollars a year, a fraction of what their sex worker patients make. Health inspectors make much less, and rumors of payoffs and bribes abound.

Regulation, while intrusive and not free of corruption, benefits individual legal sex workers in terms of the additional medical services they receive and occasional (but inconsistent) skills training on condom use, STI prevention, and HIV/AIDS. According to my findings, regulation appears to encourage more consistent health-protective behaviors, such as less condom breakage, more frequent checkups, HIV testing, and so forth, and is correlated with better health outcomes, such as a lower incidence of STI and HIV/AIDS, drug addiction, and occupational violence; in addition, it leads to a lower likelihood to engage in behaviors that place sex workers at risk, for example, trading sex for drugs, food, or shelter, having sex with HIV-positive partners, intravenous drug-using partners, or bisexual partners, or having sex while under the influence of drugs or alcohol. As legal workers, sex workers in the formal sector are given a legal health card that discourages police harassment, promotes health-protective behaviors, and allows them to work in the safest and most lucrative establishments.

Illegal Workers

There is no estimate of the number of illegal workers in Tijuana. Given the economic instability and low quality of life for the majority of its 1.5 million inhabitants, it is likely that the number far exceeds those who are legal, especially if those who work part time are included. Customers and health care workers I spoke with assumed that illegal workers worked sporadically, had fewer customers than those who were legal, were safer because they had fewer customers, and either weren't a concern in terms of public health intervention or were too difficult to identify.

I had no problem identifying illegal sex workers for this book, although getting them to participate in the project was difficult, as many were suspicious of my intentions. I found no correlation between registration status and number of clients; that is, illegal sex workers appear to have just as many customers as legal sex workers. In fact, because they often make less per client, they may need a higher turnover in clients to make the same amount of money as someone who works legally. It should not be assumed that those sex workers with the largest clientele base are legal and receive mandatory health screenings.

It is more likely that illegal sex workers represent the most vulnerable portion of the population, and they are overlooked by official accounts precisely because of the severity of the problem. Rather than being a target for outreach by health inspectors, most illegal workers are targeted by police. Unless they work in a licensed establishment with legal workers, illegal workers will be treated as criminals. The everyday experience of policing among illegal workers is characterized by incarceration, fines, police harassment, violence, rape, prejudice, discrimination, and greed, adding to their occupational risks.

According to my findings, the criminalized status of illegal sex workers shapes a number of factors that affect occupational risks, including work practices, risk priorities, risk behaviors, ability to negotiate and avoid risks, and overall health and well-being. As a result of their criminal status, many of the sex workers in the informal sector had to remain mobile in order to avoid detection by police and were less likely to be familiar with the social and physical geography of the work site, less likely to have a stable social network, and less likely to have repeat customers. If caught, they had to deal with police harassment, violence, and extortion in order to keep from going to jail. They were sometimes forced to charge less for their services, were less likely to engage in long-term economic planning, less likely to have a savings account, and less likely to be able to support other family members or their children. Because of their general vulnerability, which was increased by their criminal status, they were also more likely to have sex for drugs, food, or shelter and more likely to respond to the economic incentive to have sex without condoms.

In comparing the health behaviors and outcomes of legal and illegal workers, I found that illegal workers were also:

1. less likely to report violence because of hostile relationships with police and fear that they will be sent to jail or fined for their work activities;
2. less likely to carry condoms, for fear that police will find them and know that they are sex workers;
3. less likely to disclose their activities to regular sexual partners (noncustomers);
4. less likely to disclose their activities to health care providers;
5. less likely to be targeted by city clinic, outreach programs, and researchers;
6. less likely to have the economic resources needed for quality health care;
7. more likely to have STIs and less likely to have them treated;
8. more likely to suffer from work-related stress and depressive symptoms; and
9. more likely to suffer from drug and alcohol addiction.

Although regulation is by its nature a form of social control, sex workers' bodies are also controlled by police when they are working illegally. Thus, workers in the formal sector are policed, so to speak, by health inspectors, while most of those working in the informal sector are policed by the police. Although registration is a legal requirement of all sex workers, only female and "female-like" transgender sex workers have been targeted by inspection efforts. Thus, transgender and male workers (as I discuss more fully later) are more likely than female workers to continue to work illegally. Transgender workers and male workers are treated as potential criminals who need to be controlled by police rather than as legitimate workers who deserve protection and health services. This reflects a historical cultural norm that tends to favor control of females under the guise of protection and of males through physical aggression. Transgender workers appear to elicit both responses.

Transgender workers are targeted both by health inspectors, who try to get them to register, and by police, who harass them for being involved in drugs, for cross-dressing, and for working illegally. Male sex workers, who work in Zona Norte and elsewhere, are not targeted by health inspectors at all but are targeted by the police. No male workers are legal, that is, registered at the city clinic, and I was told by health inspectors that they had no plans to visit the gay bars, parks, or beaches where the men work in order to encourage them to register. The city health clinic does not officially acknowledge that male sex workers, who usually have gay male customers, exist. As the primary clinician explained, there is no way the city is going to acknowledge or legitimate homosexual behavior among its residents. Targeting, identifying, and holding male sex workers accountable for working illegally and encouraging them to register to work legally is seen as condoning their activities. Apparently, social tolerance of homosexual behavior among men is lower than tolerance of sex work among women. While sex between men defies gender role norms, sexual services offered to men by women and the exchange of resources from men to women reflect more socially normative patterns found among everyday residents. This is evidenced by the lack of interest in prosecuting male customers, who are seen as relatively harmless and normal and only doing what "comes naturally" (to men). It is the woman who bears the brunt of the social stigma for this exchange, for she is not under the control of a father or husband, is making her own choices in terms of her sexual partners, and is (sometimes) able to control the terms of the transaction. Female sex workers thus represent the ultimate threat to the social order, which defines true womanhood as self-sacrificing, submissive, and sexually passive.

Though male sex workers are not targeted by health inspectors, they are frequently targeted by police, especially if they are working on the street. In some cases, it is difficult to tell if their problems with police are related directly to their work or to their suspected involvement in petty crimes and drug use on the street. I examine this issue in more detail in chapter 6.

Although the benefits of regulation surpass those of criminalization, the system of health card registration is both coercive and misleading. It is coercive in that it treats sex workers as a particular type of people, people whose private lives are made public, whose bodies are subject to regulation, and who are important only insofar as they present a threat to the public health of the community or tarnish the image of the city. It is misleading in that it appears to address the needs of sex workers by providing health services, when in reality these particular services do not address the risk priorities of sex workers, such as occupational violence, police brutality, stress, depressive symptoms, and drug addiction. In addition, it neglects those who are most in need of its services, namely, males, transgenders, youth, the drug addicted, and undocumented workers working in the informal sector.

Legal Status and Occupational Risk

In order to assess whether registration status, which I use as a proxy for legal status, reflected an overall level of vulnerability, I asked my participants a set of questions about their living situations over the past few years. I believe that those who work illegally are already in a marginalized and more difficult position than those who register to work legally and that involvement in the sex industry on an illegal basis further compromises their already precarious position. Accordingly, those who have registered to work legally may already have significant advantages over those who have not registered, and their involvement in the sex industry as legally registered workers may enhance their economic stability and ability to avoid and negotiate occupational risks.

My research shows significant statistical differences between those who are registered (hereafter, Registered Female Sex Workers, or RFSW) and those who are not registered (hereafter Unregistered Female Sex Workers, or UFSW). Female sex workers who work illegally are more vulnerable than those who work legally in that they are more likely to have not had a place to stay in the past three years ($p<.07$), more likely to live and work on the streets, more likely to have been incarcerated, more likely to start sex work at an earlier age ($p<.057$), and more likely to have exchanged sex for food, shelter, clothing, and luxury items such as cell phones, perfume, and makeup (see table 5.1). Those who work legally appear to have a more stable financial situation. UFSW, who are more likely to be young, homeless, and drug addicted, exert less control over their work lives than RFSW. Taking workplace violence, work-related mental health, alcohol and drug use and addiction, sexual practices, and reproductive health outcomes as examples, I show that UFSW and RFSW clearly differ in terms of the degree and quality of unmet needs related to their work. Sex workers' narratives illustrate the context of occupational risks and are suggestive of how legal status shapes the health outcomes of the two groups.

Occupational Violence

Experiencing violence in the workplace is not uncommon for female sex workers, regardless of whether they are working legally or illegally; approximately 31 percent had experienced physical violence while at work (see table 5.2). Over 20 percent had been raped at work, and over 7 percent had been strangled, stabbed, or shot. The prevalence of particular forms of violence and the ways in which workplace violence is managed appear to be different in the two groups.

RFSW and UFSW differ from one another with respect to workplace violence in a number of complicated ways. First, although there are no significant differences between RFSW and UFSW in having been exposed to violence at least once in the workplace, UFSW are likely to have been exposed more often.[3] Second, RFSW are nearly twice as likely to report violence to authori-

Table 5.1. Signs of Vulnerability (by Legal Status)

	RFSW	UFSW
Homeless in the last three years	12%	26%
Had been incarcerated	21%	29%
Average age at first commercial sex transaction	23.4	21.4
Earliest age at first commercial sex transaction	16	12
Time since first commercial transaction (years)	4.1	3.7
Work primarily on the streets/outdoors	15%	24%
Average fee charged for vaginal sex	$92	$88
Minimum charge for vaginal sex	$13	$7
Average fee charged for oral sex	$65	$58
Minimum charge for oral sex	$38	$10
Average fee charged for anal sex	$164	*$76
Minimum charge for anal sex	$90	$10
Average number of customers a week (SD**)	7(8)	8(14)
Had exchanged sex for food	—	5%
Had exchanged sex for shelter	—	8%
Had exchanged sex for clothing	9%	2%
Had exchanged sex for luxury items	6%	10%

*p<.05
**SD = Standard Deviation

ties. Third, nearly one out of four UFSW have experienced violence at the hands of police; they are more than three times as likely to experience violence by police as RFSW. Fourth, UFSW were more likely to have experienced threats, slaps, kicks, robbery, or kidnapping than RFSW. In fact, robbery and kidnapping were twice as common for UFSW as for RFSW. One form of violence, that inflicted by an employer, while not statistically significant, does indicate that RFSW are more likely to be exposed to it than UFSW (p<.07), possibly because some RFSW actually have employers while UFSW were primarily working for and by themselves.

Police Violence

Not all sex workers fall victim to police violence: some are able to use their connections with police and civic authorities to avoid the risks associated with their profession. Legal and illegal workers have very distinct relationships

Table 5.2. Occupational Violence (by Legal Status) (percentages)

	RFSW	UFSW
Experienced workplace violence	36	30
Of those experiencing workplace violence . . .		
. . . Violence was *not* reported to police	75	87
Violence was committed by:		
Police	8	25
A customer	92	84
An employer	8	—
A stranger	25	22
Type of violence:		
Threatened	42	59
Slapped or kicked	17	31
Robbed	17	34
Kidnapped	8	16

with police. Legal workers are more likely to be aware of their rights with respect to the police. They are told by staff at the city clinic that as long as their health card remains valid, they will not be prosecuted. Within the formal sector, the relationship with the police is more amicable, as police act more like security guards for workers and help control customers. Illegal workers, on the other hand, have a far more contentious relationship with the police. They are subject to fines and jail time because they are working illegally. Police are able to take advantage of them by forcing them to pay large bribes to prevent prosecution, and they take advantage of them sexually without fear of prosecution.

Illegal workers are three times more likely than legal workers to experience police violence, intimidation, and extortion (25 percent compared to 8 percent). Because of their illegal status, they are easy prey—they are not likely to report extortion, abuse, or even rape, for fear of going to jail. They are even less likely to report abuse by law enforcement to other police because they have already experienced their corruption firsthand. They may fear further retaliation. For these workers, fear of abuse by police contributes to the dehumanizing work environment they experience:

> The very work on the street, it dehumanizes me because I am on exhibit like a thing for sale, facing dangers and being subjected to humiliations and being frightened and the abuse by the police. (Yizel, twenty-three, transgender sex worker who once worked illegally)

Even legal workers have occasionally had problems with the police, either early in their career, before they had the necessary documents to obtain a health card, or when working with an expired health card:

> I worked illegally in Cancún and was assaulted twice by the police. I did not have my nationality papers. And I could not report them because I was not a legal resident. I paid a bribe. I have also had ten customers who were very rough with me, and I could not report them for the same reason. (Alicia, twenty-eight, registered female sex worker reflecting on what it was like to work illegally)

> Once, I forgot to return [to the city clinic] for a health stamp. The police threatened to take me and nine other girls to jail, but they let us go with a warning and a 2,000 pesos fine ($US 220). (Aimara, nineteen, registered female sex worker reflecting on what it was like to work illegally, with an expired card)

Legal workers tend to have different relationships with police. Several of the sex workers I met had customers in the police force. Among legal workers, police acted as security guards for the neighborhood; as long as their cards were valid, workers rarely had any problems with them. In this situation, it was customers who bore the brunt of police attention, surveillance, and hostility. Police regularly shook down various establishments, forcing customers to stand against a wall while they were searched for drugs. The police were also on hand to settle disputes between workers and customers. Thus, for legal workers, the policing of customers offers protection against customer violence:

> Because there are persons that because they are paying you, they want to humiliate you. There are persons that on the street they talk to you very sweetly but in the room they want to abuse you. (They want to do it from behind or they do not want to use a condom.) They get angry and they leave. Most of them are cool. The police come by here a lot, and if the client gets angry he just leaves. He does not hit you. It is worse in the U.S. (Michelle, twenty-one, registered female sex worker)

> I just work for the money, but vaginal sex only. Not oral, nor anal. I have no problems because of this with the manager, but sometimes there are some clients that get violent because of this so they get their money back from me and go. Sometimes it happens because some customers want to have

sex without condoms, and they try to take it [the condom] away. When they get violent, we just call the police. One day, one man, after being with me, he tried to go away without paying for the service just because I didn't want to do it without a condom. So we called the police and they made him pay double or he was gonna go to the jail and pay the fine. And he did pay double. (Soledad, twenty-two, registered female sex worker)

Forcing a customer to pay double is a common practice, especially if that customer happens to be from the United States. The Tijuana police are notorious for taking advantage of both Tijuana residents, who are unlikely to have much money, and U.S. tourists, who are likely to have substantially more money. On the spot traffic fines are the most common tactic—people are encouraged to pay on the spot just to make the problem go away, to save themselves the inconvenience of a court date, and to save themselves from going to jail. This works easily with U.S. tourists, who have heard terrifying stories of Tijuana jails—most would do anything to keep from being dragged into one. In addition, most aren't aware of their rights and are likely to submit to any intimidation tactic the police officer tries to use. In Tijuana, the police make very little money, and they use their position and the threat of jail time to make money on the side. Although a legal worker may be off-limits, illegal workers are easy prey.

Customer Violence

Customer violence is the most common form of violence faced by sex workers. Next to mental health problems associated with work, violence is the most common hazard faced in the workplace. It can also be the most deadly:

The guy put a gun to my head and forced me to perform oral sex, he made me vomit and he threw me by the side of the road. (Lupita, seventeen, unregistered transgender sex worker)

My expectation that UFSW would experience violence at the hands of customers more often than RFSW proved to be wrong. I based my initial hypothesis on the following line of reasoning: UFSW are often on their own and working in unfamiliar areas in order to escape detection by the police. As a result, they have fewer social ties among fellow workers on the street and hotel staff and a higher likelihood of having a sexual transaction with a customer in a secluded area out of doors, such as an alley, hill, or abandoned building, or in a car:

Sometimes you do not know the risks you are setting yourself up for. Getting into cars without thinking what can happen. A short time ago [I asked the name of] a young guy in a car a couple of blocks from where he had picked me up, he said "no names" and that it was better that I get out of the car because he had a weapon and he did not want to harm me because he had liked me. (Juliana, twenty, unregistered transgender sex worker)

Although some UFSW work near persons known to them or work certain areas with friends, they are less likely than RFSW to have regular access to people who can help them prevent or address customer violence. Unlike hotel and bar staff, who are positioned at key areas, companions, who are often engaged in their own sex work activities and are not necessarily within hearing distance if something goes wrong, are not necessarily available to help defuse potential customer violence and hence it is perilous to rely on them. Over time, sex workers may be less likely to confront customers who don't want to wear condoms, who don't want to pay their asking price, or who want sexual services like anal sex that they don't want to provide—primarily because they fear violent retribution on the part of the customer and therefore feel less capable of negotiating transactions on their own terms.

Risk of customer violence appears to be shared equally by UFSW and RFSW. However, it bears repeating that RFSW are twice as likely as UFSW to report violence to the police. Additionally, UFSW reported having experienced incidents of customer violence an average of three times since they had started sex work. The ability to deal with perpetrators through the authorities, and hold them accountable for their actions is a privilege that those working illegally do not have access to. Abusive customers can take advantage of UFSW, knowing it is unlikely they will be reported to the police.

Robbery is a particular problem among street workers, who are led into more private areas by potential customers and are mugged at knife or gunpoint or who have sex with customers who refuse to pay them (which is also a form of rape).[4] Some customers refused to pay or threatened violence if they did not get their money back. According to the workers, customers did made such threats when they felt dissatisfied and entitled to make the sex worker give them their money back. The most common reason cited was that the customer had not achieved orgasm in the time allotted him. The high level of robbery involved in customer transactions with illegal workers may indicate that the economic status of their customers is less stable and that the nature of their transactions allows more room for opportunistic theft. Although legal sex workers, who work at the top of the social hierarchy, are able to charge more money per transaction, the illegal street worker might be seen as a safer robbery target. Illegal workers are less likely to have a safe place to store their money, and the transaction requires less socializing, is less visible, and does not require buying drinks in order to pass as a paying customer. It is unlikely someone in need of money will enter a bar or massage parlor to rob a sex worker, as it is more dangerous than robbing an illegal worker in an informal setting. UFSW may be seen as targets who are unlikely to go to the police and as less worthy of respect. Thus, although customer violence is high regardless of legal status, particular forms of violence are more prevalent depending on the setting of the transaction. More research should be conducted on these incidents in order to examine and understand the complexities involved.

Reporting Violence

One out of four RFSW reports violent incidents to police; only one out of eight UFSW reports these incidents. UFSW fear that they will be harassed, jailed, or fined by police if they report such incidents. Although the reporting rate is low overall, RFSW can utilize other work relationships in holding customers accountable for violence. This advantage is connected to the more formalized system in which their work activities take place. Legal sex workers who work in bars must pay a bar fine if they engage in sex for pay off the premises (there are half-hour and one-hour rooms available in the hotels connected to each bar). While using a connected hotel does not prevent customer violence, it does have its advantages. Hotel staff are familiar with the sex workers and monitor the time spent in rooms. They will check on the room after thirty minutes and are known to be extremely attentive, banging on the doors and sometimes barging into the room:

> One time a customer was mad because he hadn't finished and we had to leave the room, because he hadn't finished by that time he told me I was a thief and he left angry. (Ivonne, twenty, registered female sex worker)

Bouncers and doormen are also around in case a customer gets out of hand. Some sex workers have code words or sounds, like knocking on the wall, to alert hotel staff that they are in danger. The hotel staff rely on high room turnover and on tips left by the sex workers in order to make their living, so it pays to be attentive in more ways than one:

> One guy [customer] was doing coke and was upset that I couldn't get him hard. He threatened to beat the shit out of me. Another tried to rape me without a condom. Also, one young American was spanking me during sex

and calling me a bitch and a whore. But the guys [the hotel staff] came and took them. (Juana, nineteen, registered female sex worker)

Knowing the benefits of this vigilance, sex workers are unlikely to follow customers to an alternate location, primarily because they don't want to put themselves in additional danger and because of the bar fine. These arrangements are beneficial to sex worker employees, hotel staff, and management, who increase profits by requiring utilization of their hotel services. The majority of these types of hotel/bar arrangements are available only to legal sex workers—owners risk losing their license if they are caught with illegal workers too often. Legal street sex workers, most of whom dominate the streets surrounding the Coahuila district, have a similar arrangement with hotel staff and will look out for one another if a fellow worker hasn't returned to their spot when expected.

Murder Rates and Other Data

Local statistics on deaths of sex workers were not available through the police. Even if such statistics were collected, they would likely be unreliable. In Tijuana, public health and criminal statistics are generally unavailable, and those that are collected are not published. In some cases, it took me over a year to collect raw data and try to make sense of it. There are still some data I was not privy to. In the case of sources I did have access to, for example, medical record data collected by the city clinic, I was allowed to consult them and make notes on their content but not to remove them from the premises. I prepared an entire report on newly legal sex workers for the clinic but was not allowed to remove the data from the premises. In part, this was due to concerns about intellectual property—and to prior experiences with U.S.-based researchers who publish local data sources as their own. However, local residents widely approve of the actions of local civic and business leaders in withholding this type of information, which is seen as a way of protecting both the tourist industry and themselves.

Narratives about sex workers who were murdered were available to me. While these narratives don't provide a measure of the extent of this kind of violence, the retelling of the narratives communicates, expresses, and, to some extent, enhances the fear and intimidation felt by sex workers:

[I worry that] what happened to four girlfriends [will happen to me]. One was raped and was found with a rock on her head, another one was found in an abandoned house, raped by four Americans ["Gabachos"] and they strangled her. Another one, "La Amor," was found near an abandoned house and they had stuck a large stake in her "part" [vagina]. And the one in Ensenada was also raped and dismembered and they sent parts from her face and fingers to her mother. It is said that that happened to her also because she was involved in large-scale drug sales. Yet another one was raped [while going to school] and she showed up in a trash container wrapped in a sheet. This was about four months ago. (Elodia, twenty-three, unregistered female sex worker)

One sex worker, who wished to remain anonymous and didn't want her voice recorded in case she was recognized by a fellow worker or manager, told me the following story:

I think we are human beings and we deserve to be treated better. I've heard about three women who died at the hand of clients, our bosses covered it up, but the room cleaner told me about these cases and I believe him. Two of the girls' families are still looking for them. One of the girls, she was living there [at the hotel attached to the bar], they [the management] said she took everything and left. This girl was always calling home, she had kids, she would never just disappear. She was stabbed by an American client, but the managers, they have friends in the police, they control everything. I want her body to bury her, to pray for her. (anonymous, twenty-nine, registered female sex worker)

These stories were not the only ones I heard off the record. Such accounts are hard to verify,[5] but the telling of the stories indicates the overall sense of fear, intimidation, anxiety, and mental stress felt by sex workers in Tijuana:

[A] lot of news comes out about someone who was found strangled or shot the next morning for doing this and I get very tense now. (Katia, twenty, registered transgender sex worker)

The psychological dimensions of physical violence are far more extensive than any available statistics or quotations can illustrate. Other aspects of their work also have psychological costs.

Occupational Stress and Depressive Symptoms

Stress and depressive symptoms related to work were cited more frequently than any other work-related health problem (table 5.3). Mental health prob-

Table 5.3. Stress and Depressive Symptoms (by Legal Status) (percentages)

	RFSW	UFSW
Average number of symptoms (ten-point scale)	N=5	N=6
Felt symptoms were connected to work	75	*84
Types of symptoms:		
Sadness	71	*82
Loss of interest/pleasure	36	*49
Change in appetite	61	*70
Change in sleeping patterns	61	66
Anxiety	71	**50
Loss of energy	46	*55
Feelings of shame/guilt	75	*84
Difficulty concentrating	50	*60
Loss of libido	42	*53
Suicidal thoughts	7	*25

Mean (SD); *p<.05; **p<.01

lems cut across all sex worker subgroups, regardless of gender or legal status. Some generalizations about mental health issues can be made about all of the sex workers participating in this study; there are also differences between those who work legally and illegally as well as differences based on gender. Not only did the vast majority (75–84 percent) feel a strong causal relationship between their work and their experience of these symptoms, many experienced nine out of ten of these symptoms daily and unrelentingly. Recurring thoughts of suicide were common, and the sense of having limited options was particularly traumatic:

> [When I did not like the person], I would feel very depressed, dirty. I felt very bad. But mostly I did it for the money and to dress and buy shoes. I felt like committing suicide. (Rosita, twenty-one, unregistered female sex worker)

The perceived lack of sexual agency and control at work can parallel and reinforce the trauma associated with early sexual experiences in childhood or the trauma associated with sexual assault:

> Since I was a girl I do not like being touched by men I do not like. It depresses me that now I do it for my children. I think I need to see a psychia-

trist or someone who will help me with this depression. I cannot stand it. (Pasha, twenty-four, registered female sex worker)

Sex workers' mental health is shaped by varying degrees of economic need and sexual and personal agency. Perceptions of self-efficacy, agency, and personal autonomy shape the meanings associated with sex work transactions and the impact these activities have on health and quality of life:

> It all goes hand in hand. Sometimes if there was a lot of clientele, my self-esteem was high, I felt well because there was more money coming in. I felt more wanted. When there was nothing, everything sort of went down. It was as if I was not wanted or I felt I was not appealing to anyone. (Xenia, twenty-one, unregistered transgender sex worker)

To identify potential differences in the extent of various depressive symptoms between legal and illegal sex workers I used a modified version of the Beck Depression Inventory—Short Form for rapid assessment (Beck et al. 1974) translated into Spanish. Each respondent was asked if they had experienced the symptoms daily for more than two weeks prior to the interview. During this portion of the interview, many commented that they had felt these symptoms for more than a few months, some for a few years. Considering their shared experiences of working with increased exposure to violence and the daily threat of violence, this finding is not surprising. What is surprising is that mental health needs among sex workers have not been recognized as a significant public health need that should be addressed. Violence, substance abuse, and work-related mental health problems are all far more prevalent than STIs, play a role in increased risk behaviors resulting in greater incidence of STIs, and yet are completely ignored by the municipal authorities charged with public health and safety. As I will demonstrate, the psychological consequences of social stigma combined with substandard and hazardous working conditions are clearly demoralizing.

Social stigma has a significant impact on sex workers' mental health. Stigma can increase fear and anxiety associated with being "found out":

> You feel ashamed that your friends might find out or tell you that you went with someone for money. It is sad, it makes you feel you are worthless, it lowers your self-esteem. I am ashamed to work here. I do not want my family to know what I do. Nor my children. (Esmeralda, twenty-nine, unregistered female sex worker)

The stigma of being a sex worker can be compounded by other kinds of social stigma. In some cases, the social stigma attached to sexual orientation, disability, or being extremely poor can limit alternatives to sex work. The sense of desperation caused by factors not related to sex work can make the experience of sex work all the more devastating:

> Sometimes I feel revulsion doing things I do not want with clients just for the money. I feel very lonely, without support from my family, that is why I do this. I try to look for a "normal" job and they do not want me for being gay or they pay miserable wages. (Paco, nineteen, unregistered male sex worker)

Legal status can shape the meaning attached to sex work activities (defining them as socially legitimate or criminal), as can the kinds of work experiences and working conditions faced by sex workers. As the table illustrates, depressive symptoms are common among both subgroups but are an average of 10 percent more frequent among illegal workers in nearly every category. In addition, one out of four illegal workers had recurring thoughts of suicide or had attempted suicide in the two weeks prior to the survey. Legal sex workers reported that their legal status provided some measure of personal esteem as well as greater control over their working conditions. Legal workers are not treated in the same way illegal workers are; they are offered protections and professional respect that illegal workers do not enjoy. These factors may explain why mental health problems are more common and more severe among those working illegally.

Of all the sections in the survey, this one was the most difficult for participants to answer. Feeling that the questions hit too close to home, nine chose not to respond at all, making it difficult (because of the smaller population size) to assess the statistical significance of the differences between legal and illegal workers. Their explanations for not answering, however, indicate the significant impact sex work can have on the mind, body, and spirit:

> The work does depress me. I think about my life before and the one I have now. I did not do this before. I do not want to answer anymore. (Leandra, twenty-three, registered female sex worker)

As I discuss in the next section, many described these symptoms as motivations for getting high and drinking alcohol. HIV prevention that targets risk reduction as a protective health behavior is likely to be a challenge with this group until these needs have been addressed. Treatment of depression and possible post traumatic stress disorder would likely decrease the risk of HIV infection among these participants and lead to greater quality of life overall. However, clinical treatment cannot be done in isolation. It has been shown repeatedly that early exposure to trauma can increase the likelihood of work-related trauma and poor health and mental health outcomes among sex workers (Cwikel et al. 2004).

Increasing social supports, reducing the social stigma associated with sex work, reducing violence in the workplace, providing substance abuse treatment, and providing counseling to work through the trauma associated with physical and sexual assault on the job (or during childhood or with intimate sexual partners) are all measures that would have a profound impact on sex workers' mental health. Although these measures would reduce the harm associated with the industry, a more preferable long-term solution is to create viable alternatives to sex work. In recognition of the psychological and physical impacts of sex work, public policymakers must ensure that no one decides to engage in sex work because they have no viable alternatives. As I show in the following section, the impact of living with a "forced choice" may encourage a variety of coping strategies, including alcohol and drug use, which are a further detriment to physical and mental health.

Substance Use and Addiction

Substance use is both a coping strategy and a motivation for entry into sex work. Substance use was common among both legal and illegal sex workers, but much more so among illegal workers (table 5.4). Hostile interactions with the police, unstable working environments, mental stress, and greater stigma increase the likelihood of substance use and addiction among illegal sex workers:

> I have to use drugs to go out. To give myself the courage to do what I do and face everything the police do to [us] every day and so very often. (Marlina, twenty, unregistered transgender sex worker)

Illegal workers are more likely to engage in illegal drug use than legal workers, thereby compounding their problems with the police. They are nearly twice as likely to have exchanged sex for drugs, and they are more than eight times more likely to have engaged in sex work while on drugs. They also begin using drugs at an earlier age; they are more prone to using a greater variety of drugs

Table 5.4. Alcohol and Illicit Drug Use (by Legal Status) (percentages)

	RFSW	*UFSW*
Age at which they first got drunk (mean)	19 years	*17 years
Frequently drink to get drunk	64	50
Think they have a drinking problem	3	7
Frequently have sex while drunk	42	34
Have sex to get alcohol	6	2
Age at which they first used illicit drugs (mean)	23 years	20 years
Frequently use drugs to get high	21	36
Think they have a drug problem	6	16
Frequently have sex while on drugs	21	32
Have sex for drugs	—	12
Types of drugs used:		
Methamphetamine	18	21
Marijuana	15	13
Cocaine	12	22
Heroin	—	13
Crack-cocaine	—	3
Inhalants (paint, glue, etc.)	—	<1
Other drugs (pills)	—	3

*p<.05

and nearly three times more likely to develop an addiction. Their two most popular drugs, crystal methamphetamine ("crystal" or "crank") and cocaine, are two of the most addictive drugs available. They are popular with all sex workers in Tijuana, as they are both appetite suppressants, helping to keep the body slim for customers, and energy enhancers, allowing them to stay up late and service more customers.

There is a significant difference between RFSW and UFSW with respect to how old they were when they first drank to get drunk (p<.04). UFSW are likely to be much younger than RFSW when they first drink to get drunk. This may indicate that UFSW are less socially stable at younger ages than RFSW, are exposed to alcohol use at younger ages, and possibly more likely to self-medicate with alcohol at a younger age. In addition, although binge drinking is more common among RFSW,[6] UFSW are more than twice as likely to report that they have a problem with alcohol addiction. The picture is similar with respect to drug use.

Table 5.5. Needle Use (by Legal Status) (percentages)

	RFSW	UFSW
Report needle use for vitamin injection	33	32
...Use only store-bought needles	100	100
Report needle use for illicit drugs	3	12
...Injected drugs (past six months)	—	92
Report sharing needles	8	38
...Use bleach to clean needles	100	40
...Use water or don't clean needles	—	60

UFSW start taking drugs an average of about three years earlier than RFSW. They are also twelve times more likely to exchange sex for drugs or for money to buy drugs. In addition, UFSW use drugs with more frequency than RFSW, are nearly twice as likely to have used drugs in the past six months, and nearly three times more likely to have used them in the past week. They are 70 percent more likely than RFSW to have sex while high, and four times more likely to always get high before engaging in sexual intercourse. They are nearly three times more likely to think they have a problem with drugs. Last, although UFSW and RFSW are similar in terns of their use of methamphetamines and marijuana, UFSW are thirteen times more likely to use heroin, three times more likely to use crack or prescription drugs, twice as likely to use inhalants, and nearly twice as likely to use cocaine. No female sex worker reported using ecstasy.

The use of needles to inject vitamins is fairly common among both UFSW and RFSW (see table 5.5). Vitamin injection is common among the general population, and one out of three sex workers engages in this practice regardless of legal status. Vitamins and needles are packaged together and are easily purchased without prescription in Mexico. However, because new needles are now used for each vitamin injection and there is no need to share needles, needle use in vitamin injections does not appear to pose any risk for either UFSW or RFSW. This is a change from how vitamins were injected before the AIDS epidemic; new packaging of needles with the vitamins appears to have limited HIV infections resulting from sharing of needles for vitamin injections. With respect to illicit drug use, however, UFSW are four times more likely than RFSW to inject drugs and are more likely to do so in a way that puts them at risk for blood-borne pathogens like Hepatitis B, Hepatitis C, or HIV. While the one RFSW that was once an Injection Drug User (IDU) had not injected within the past six months, nearly all (92 percent) of the UFSW had done so. They are nearly five times more likely to report sharing needles with others. The one RFSW who reported sharing needles also reported cleaning the needle with bleach before sharing. She may have been exposed to public health professionals and the city clinic, which has posters and brochures on safe needle practices located throughout the clinic. Of the five UFSW who reported sharing needles, only two used bleach to clean them—the rest used water or didn't clean them at all.

More research is necessary to determine why UFSW use alcohol and drugs at an earlier age, with greater frequency, and with greater associated risk practices. Whether as a result of needing to cope with more hazardous working conditions as a result of their illegal status, deeper involvement in street culture and drug dealers, or problems with drug and alcohol addiction prior to their involvement in sex work (and perhaps as a motivation for sex work), working illegally is clearly correlated with drug and alcohol use, possibly in more ways than one. Given the extent of work-related psychological and physical stressors, the greater likelihood of work-related stressors, and the unmet mental health needs of UFSW, it is not unexpected that they would have unmet needs that might lead to more extensive self-medication through drug and alcohol use. The precise nature of these connections as well as the role of causal factors could be examined more closely through additional research, particularly through the use of a more detailed combination of life history and drug use trajectories.

Sexually Transmitted Infections (STIs): Testing and Treatment Issues

The system of health card registration affords a level of protection to those who are legal through regular access to testing services and health education. However, this system is inadequate for a number of reasons. First, except for the blood test given for syphilis, STI screening at the city clinic is not done through laboratory tests. Only visible symptoms are given attention. This is problematic because symptoms are not always visible or may be visible only at certain times during the infection. Under this system, then, sex workers may believe they are free of infection (and thus incapable of infecting others) when they are not, and as a result they may not receive treatment for STIs that are present. Such misdiagnoses could very well make them sterile or generate higher risk of further infection, including infection with HIV. In addition, the measurement of STIs by the city clinic is inaccurate and misleading, as the rates of visible infections are likely to be much lower than rates of actual infections. Furthermore, the city clinic is not required to disclose what STIs it screens for, which can be confusing to those who receive regular STI checkups and stamps of approval.

STIs like chlamydia and genital tuberculosis, which are virtually undetectable by visual exam yet are known to be present by the doctors at the clinic, aren't ever treated or screened for. Chlamydia, for example, is the most common STI in the United States, affecting over three million people every year (CDC 2001), and has been shown to be the most common STI among sex workers in Durango, Mexico (16.6 percent tested positive for it) (Alvarado-Esquivel et al. 2000). Chlamydia is likely a major health risk among sex workers in Tijuana; however, no epidemiological surveillance or screenings for the infection are available in the clinic. This is particularly troubling because chlamydia can lead to infertility, pelvic inflammatory disease, and a three-to-five-times increased risk for HIV infection. Genital tuberculosis, a condition noted by the clinic's doctors to be present among sex workers, has never been screened for at the clinic. However, given that rates of other forms of tuberculosis are prevalent and of concern all along the border, it makes sense that this condition exists and should be screened for. STI treatment and screening and high-risk sexual practices are serious issues in terms of personal safety and occupational risks as well as valid public health concerns. STIs not only cause debilitating pain, death, and sterility, but also are known to increase risk for infection with the HIV virus.[7] Table 5.6 illustrates the distribution of behaviors that play a role in increased risk for STI. While the incidence of new STI symptoms in legal and illegal workers was similar over the prior six months, the actual prevalence of STIs in both subpopulations is unknown, as comprehensive testing for either population does not take place (see table 5.6). Treatment and screening for STI and HIV are less prevalent among illegal workers than among legal workers. All legal workers receive mandatory screening for at least some STIs, and 100 percent of those who needed treatment received it before being allowed to work legally. Only 11 percent had not yet received an HIV test, but 100 percent would have received an HIV test through the city clinic within four months (for some reason the first test is not given until after the newly legal worker has been engaged in sex work for four months; presumably this is based on the faulty assumption that HIV infection is likely to occur through work and not prior to registration).

Among illegal workers, STI treatment and screening were less common. One out of five had experienced symptoms of an STI but had not sought treatment. Because they were not involved in a regular screening program, they had less knowledge overall about the potential harm of STIs, including increased risk for HIV infection. Over half hadn't visited a doctor in more

Table 5.6. Sexually Transmitted Infections (by Legal Status) (percentages)

	RFSW	UFSW
STI screening in the past year	94	*47
HIV/AIDS test in the past year	91	**55
Symptoms of an STI (past six months)	27	23
Had symptoms and obtained treatment	100	72
Believed they were HIV-negative	88	**51
Believed they were HIV-positive	—	**<1
Weren't sure about HIV status	12	**49
Tested HIV-positive in this study	—	5

*p<.0001; **p<.001

than a year and slightly less than half had never received an HIV/AIDS test. Although both legal and illegal workers used condoms to reduce the risk of contracting STIs, condom use was fraught with difficulties and was less widely accepted among illegal than legal workers (see below).

Use of private doctors and clinics to treat STIs was high among both legal and illegal sex workers. Of those who sought treatment for an STI, 92 percent had gone to a private doctor or clinic rather than to a pharmacist or traditional healer. This is a significant finding because the tradition of medical pluralism in Mexico is quite strong, as is the use of pharmacists, who eliminate the cost and time spent on a doctor's visit but still provide a prescription. It may be that STIs fall into a category of diseases that are regarded as best treated by a physician. Although no comparative data were available, my sense is that Tijuana sex workers resort to medical professionals for STI treatment more often than residents who are not sex workers, who often cannot afford such treatment or don't understand the nature of STI detection and treatment.

Condom Use with Customers

Sex workers in Tijuana report that they regularly use condoms to prevent pregnancy, STIs, and HIV/AIDS. Reported condom use by sex workers and their customers was very high among both legal and illegal workers (100 percent and 96 percent, respectively), much higher than reports from countries where all sex work is illegal and about the same as those areas where sex work is regulated.[8] Table 5.7 illustrates condom use patterns and HIV/AIDS-related sexual practices among RFSW and UFSW in Tijuana. Condom use was more prevalent among both legal and illegal females than among males and illegal

Table 5.7. Condom Use and Sexual Practices (by Legal Status) (percentages)

	RFSW	UFSW
Reported 100% condom use	100	98
Used a condom with last customer	100	98
Friends always use condoms	27	21
Problems negotiating condom use	12	6
Always places condom on customer themselves	82	79
Condom breakage (past month)	33	34
Uses lubricants with condoms	61	46
... Oil-based lubricants	—	6
... Any lubricant (whatever is convenient)	—	12
... Only water or silicone-based	100	83
One or more noncommercial partners	66	64
... Partner is known to be HIV-positive	—	<1
... Partner is known to be an intravenous drug user	15	16
... Partner is known to be bisexual	52	36
Living with partner	33	28
Have had only male sexual partners	91	93
Identify as heterosexual	100	95
Identify as bisexual	—	5

transgender workers. This indicates that although legal and illegal sex workers acknowledge the importance of condom use in terms of occupational safety, gender, sexual orientation, and social norms may complicate matters. Gender and age may be far more important than legal status in shaping patterns of condom use.

Unlike legal workers, illegal workers were far more likely to allow the customers to place the condom, to use oil-based lubricants with latex condoms, and to experience condom breakage. As Sowadsky (1999) notes,

> People will use almost anything as a lubricant when having sex. . . . Crisco, butter, hand lotion, K-Y, Wet, Astroglide, water, spit/saliva, shampoo, soap, mineral oil, whipped cream, jam/jellies, toothpaste, shaving cream, mouth-wash, semen . . . you name it. If it feels slippery, people will use it as a lubricant (Internet site, no page number).

Lubricants can make sexual intercourse more pleasurable; some lubricants, like K-Y, Astroglide, and saliva, can reduce the likelihood not only that the vagina will sustain abrasions during intercourse, but also that the condom will break, thereby providing additional protection against STIs and HIV. Of the legal workers I spoke with, 57 percent used a water-based lubricant in addition to latex condoms when having sexual intercourse with a customer. Only 39 percent of illegal sex workers did so. Other lubricants, like toothpaste, shaving cream, and mouthwash, can cause genital irritation and increase the risk for STIs. Oil-based lubricants damage latex products, and only water-based lubricants can be used safely with latex condoms. No legal sex workers who participated in this study used oil-based lubricants with latex condoms, while 6 percent of illegal sex workers used oil-based lubricants and an additional 1 percent used lubricants of an unknown composition.[9] In speaking with both groups of workers, I learned that while the proper use of lubricants was discussed at both the city clinic and, more informally, at sex workers' union meetings, most of those working illegally were not aware of the differences and dangers of the various kinds of lubricants.[10] The disparity indicates that illegal workers are less familiar with appropriate safer sex strategies than legal workers, probably because they don't receive regular health intervention and training by the city clinic.

Allowing customers to place the condom can potentially increase the risk for STI. They may be less experienced than the worker, placing the condom incorrectly or tearing it. Such circumstances can make the condom less effective as a barrier for STI. Because of the sizable number of partners most sex workers have had and the greater chance they have been shown how to use a condom correctly by other sex workers or by health care workers, sex workers are best prepared for condom placement. They are better able to protect themselves and their customers. Condom placement requires that the worker have a greater degree of control over the transaction, and it is probable that illegal sex workers experience a lesser degree of control because of their illegal status and the clandestine nature of the transaction. Nearly twice as many illegal workers as legal chose to allow their customer to place the condom (30 percent and 17 percent, respectively). I believe that the consequences of this decision explain in part the higher monthly rate of condom breakage among illegal workers (36 percent) than among legal workers (26 percent). Identifying the exact rate per transaction, which would require careful recording on a daily basis, was outside the scope of this study. Thus, the monthly incidence rate should not be confused with the incidence rate per sexual transaction. Although my participants had trouble estimating the number of sexual partners they had each month, they definitely had more sexual encounters than non–sex workers, averaging about fifty customers per month. An educated guess at the rate per transaction would then equate to less than 1 percent for both groups.

In similar studies, the condom breakage rate per sexual encounter among non–sex workers is just under 5 percent (Richters et al. 1995) but is much lower among sex workers, especially brothel-based workers. Among legal sex workers, condom breakage was 0 percent among Nevada brothel-based sex workers (Albert et al. 1995), 0.8 percent in the Netherlands (de Graaf et al. 1993), and around 1 percent among brothel-based workers in Singapore (Wong et al. 2000). On the basis of their research, de Graaf et al. argue that "condom quality was seldom reported as the cause; breakage was generally attributed to human factors, such as rough or prolonged intercourse, incorrect handling of the condom or the use of insufficient lubricant . . . [and] penis size" (1993: 265). However, these human factors can be overcome through additional experience and tips from fellow workers and health workers. According to Albert et al., "Regular condom use may lead to condom mastery and the development of techniques to reduce the likelihood of breakage and slippage" (1995: 1514). The study by Wong et al., which found that additional sex work experience decreased failure rates, supports this claim; my own findings also support this claim. In addition, they suggest that legal status, social connections with other workers, and regular interaction with city clinic workers encourage skill building with respect to reduced condom failure rates.

HIV/AIDS Infection

As noted, five female sex workers tested HIV-positive in this study (tables 5.8 and 5.9). All five worked illegally. Although primary prevention efforts for HIV/AIDS tend to focus on promoting condom use and other safer sex practices, medical and social science research has shown that those populations most vulnerable to HIV infection face serious constraints in their ability to understand risks, negotiate condom use, and avoid infection.[11] Most public policy focuses on "safer sex" practices and emphasizes self-control, self-discipline, and individual responsibility.[12] Such approaches, however, deflect attention from the socioeconomic context of sexual behavior and therefore from the systematic inequalities that complicate an individual's ability to avoid infection.[13] HIV prevention efforts that target sex workers are largely unable to deal with macrolevel, structural factors, such as gender inequality, migration, the wage system, unfair labor practices, and insufficient infrastructure. Such programs generally have only enough resources to conduct localized, neighborhood-level interventions such as condom distribution, health education, and, occasionally, civil rights abuses. By failing to address the risk priorities of sex workers, such interventions are less relevant and less significant in the lives of sex workers and in the general occupational risks they ex-

Table 5.8. Personal Profile of HIV-positive Female Sex Workers (N=5)

	Personal Profile and Demographics
5	Do not speak English
3	Cannot read or write
5	Had never been to high school
4	Had never been to junior high school
5	Have children—average number of children: five
5	Have fostered children out to family members
5	Were not born in Tijuana
3	Had been without a place to stay in past three years
3	Had been incarcerated
3	Crossed into the United States to work or visit friends
2	Send monthly remittances to family members
3	Currently have a regular sexual partner
5	Believed regular sexual partner is not HIV-positive
4	Have a partner they know to be bisexual
2	Have partner who is intravenous drug user

perience. My book is a call to policymakers to understand the context of risk for sex workers—a context which includes macrostructural factors, competing risks and risk priorities, risk management practices, and everyday experiences and meanings shared by this diverse population. It is not, therefore, only a book about the political economy of risk for HIV/AIDS, but a book about the political economy of occupational risks. Risk for STIs and HIV/AIDS, while feared and certainly managed carefully, was something that the sex workers I interviewed felt in greater control of—safer sex included a set of practices they had already learned and had less trouble managing. Yet in order to provide my participants with a valuable service that most did not have access to, I offered each one a free HIV test.

The oral fluid test used detects HIV antibodies, which become detectable only after about six months. Thus, current prevalence could not be determined (the test was cost prohibitive). Also, the incidence of new infections was not measured, as a longitudinal study tracking participants over time would have been outside the scope of my book. As a point for comparison, however, the incidence rate of new HIV infections among sex workers legalized at the city clinic was less than 1 percent (only 0.4 percent). Though it would appear that illegal sex workers are ten times more likely to become infected with HIV, this is not quite an accurate comparison—legal sex workers with HIV are removed from the system immediately, which keeps the prevalence rate at 0 percent.

Table 5.9. Work Profile of HIV-positive Female Sex Workers (N=5)

	Work Practices and Experiences
5	Work illegally
5	Work primarily on the streets
5	Use heroin daily
2	Had been raped while at work
3	Had experienced work-related police violence
5	Experienced nine of ten symptoms for depression
5	Perceived connection between depression and work
5	Had recurring thoughts of suicide
4	Had never been tested for HIV
2	Reported condom breakage in the past month
4	Do not use lubricant or use oil-based lubricants
3	Reported having had sex with more than one thousand customers
4	Reported more than one romantic relationship with customers
5	Provide vaginal sex—average fee $13
5	Provide oral sex—average fee $17
2	Provide anal sex—average fee $22

Such workers may continue to work illegally or return to their natal home; in either case, their HIV status is not tracked or counted by anyone. None of the ten HIV-positive workers I met decided to stop working after learning of their infection, and six had been tested previously. Of these six, two had learned of their serostatus prior to this particular test, two had never returned for their results, and two had tested negative but had been infected more recently. None had developed symptoms of AIDS or had received any sort of treatment. The threat of death by AIDS, while frightening, was a risk removed from their current experience. They were far more concerned with basic survival and those risks which would affect them in the short term. Because HIV/AIDS care and treatment are not provided by the government for the majority of those infected, sex work will probably become even more important as a way to afford care and treatment after the development of symptoms.

In looking at the gender differences in HIV infection among nonlegal sex workers, I found that HIV outreach might be highly important for transgender workers, whose prevalence rate was just over 21 percent. Male and female infections were both 5 percent. Female sex workers in Tijuana infrequently engage in anal sex, relying on oral or vaginal sex or both to service their customers; male sex workers in Tijuana often give anal sex to their customers, and perform or receive oral sex. However, the nature of sex work by transgenders in this study almost always included being the recipient of anal sex, known to greatly increase the risk for HIV infection.

Identifying the potential sources of transmission among these participants is not complicated, but risk for HIV infection is multilayered, and there is no one specific source for each individual. All of those who were infected with HIV engaged in multiple high-risk behaviors at home and at work, including drug and needle practices and sex with regular partners who were potentially infected or known to be infected. Many also experienced frequent condom breakage with their customers. In terms of other potential risk factors, eight of the ten HIV-positive workers used needles for hormones, vitamins, or drugs, and seven had done so in the last six months. Six out of the seven who used needles in the previous six months admitted to using heroin, five out of seven said they were drug addicted, and three reported that they had never used drugs. Eight of the ten workers reported having had a regular partner who was bisexual, five had a partner who used intravenous drugs, and two had partners who were known to be HIV positive themselves. All used condoms consistently with their customers and had used a condom with their last customer, but six had experienced condom breakage in the past month. Six used condoms with their regular partners.

According to Sacks (1996), reliable comparative rates of HIV infection between sex workers and non–sex workers are rare because of the failure to use control groups of non–sex workers, the use of outdated and inaccurate HIV tests, and the selection of populations of sex workers who are more likely to be intravenous drug users or are already engaging in unprotected sex (in jails, drug rehabilitation centers, STI clinics). Though research of this nature is highly problematic, some studies suggest that in the absence of drug addiction, HIV infection rates among sex workers and non–sex workers are virtually indistinguishable in most settings worldwide (ibid.). Evidence suggests that this is primarily because condom use with regular partners (that is, boyfriends and husbands) is rare among both sex workers and non–sex workers, whereas condom use with clients during sex work activities is much more frequent and consistent.[14] The data I collected support these claims, at least among legal sex workers.

Fifteen percent had experienced problems negotiating condom use with customers, and these experiences were slightly more prevalent among legal sex workers than illegal ones, perhaps because they were more adamant about condom use than the other workers. Concerns about personal safety and permission to work undoubtedly were factors in encouraging condom use among legal workers.

My conversations with legal sex workers suggested that greater experience in sexual services increases not only awareness of and responsibility in relation to STIs, but also sexual negotiation skills and the ability to set firm sexual boundaries. Greater experience with condoms and lubricants can also increase partner satisfaction and reduce condom breakage. All of these factors make correct, consistent condom use more likely. However, when combined with drug use, migration to an unfamiliar city, economic desperation, discrimination, inexperience, and a lack of alternatives for survival, some legal and many illegal sex workers may have difficulty avoiding infection.[15] The greater the degree of economic independence prior to entry into sex work and the greater income generated by legal sex workers, the easier to avoid infection.

The findings of this book demonstrate that sex workers are not a homogenous group in terms of legal status, age, family relations, sexual abuse, drug history, mental health status, access to health care, educational background, socioeconomic resources, family responsibilities, work preferences, or social skills. Each factor shapes sex workers' overall vulnerability. Vulnerability directly translates into an individual's knowledge, attitudes, and practices—and therefore into their risk for occupational violence, police harassment and abuse, occupational stress and depressive symptoms, and STIs, including HIV/AIDS.

As I have demonstrated, illegal workers in Tijuana are less apt than legal sex workers to receive appropriate treatment for STIs. Lack of access to health services can result in pelvic inflammatory disease, genital ulcers, open sores, and a lower immunosuppressive response, and therefore an increased risk for HIV infection.[16] Malnutrition, another health risk faced by some of the most vulnerable sex workers, inhibits production of the lubricating, protective mucus in the vagina, slows the healing process in general, and depresses the immune system—all factors which increase risk for HIV infection and AIDS-related complications (Farmer et al. 1996). Because untreated STIs raise the risk for HIV infection and can result in sterility and other reproductive health problems (for example, there is a connection between vaginal warts and increased risk for cervical cancer), more complete testing and health education are needed by illegal workers.

Because the informal sector is not a target of health outreach and services, skewed statistics distributed by the city create the impression that mandatory testing of legal workers has solved the problem of occupational risks for sex workers in Tijuana. The very structure of the services excludes from the system those sex workers who fall short of this ideal. Workers who do become positive are immediately withdrawn from the statistical pool, they are not counted, and their needs are not acknowledged or addressed by civic authorities.[17]

Testing, which should be encouraged for all residents, helps identify those most vulnerable to infection as well as reduces the risk of future health problems and their concomitant high human and financial costs. There should be safe, confidential centers for testing and health education that will work with populations who cannot or do not access services at the municipal testing center—these include such subgroups as youth sex workers, sex workers from massage parlors and call services, male sex workers, and migrant sex workers who arrive in Tijuana without proper identification and are therefore denied services. These need not be mandatory services, but they should be accessible, welcoming, and protective of sex workers.

Conclusion

Police violence has always been a problem for sex workers but has become less of a problem for legal sex workers as a result of evolving regulations and agreements among the city clinic, sex workers, and the police. On April 29, 1992, responding to police violence in the formal sector, some legal street workers in the Coahuila district formed a group called Vanguardia de Mujeres Libres María Magdalena. As a result of their activities, civic protests, and support by other social activists, the longtime members of the group have experienced a reduction in abuse and violation of human rights by the police. The newer members don't even recognize police violence as a significant problem because Las Magdalenas were so effective in stopping the violence directed toward them. They also organize STI-prevention workshops for their members, none of whom have become infected with HIV. They meet once a week and have been heavily involved in shaping the health protocols of the city clinic for sex workers. Some of their successes in this arena included mandatory private examination rooms (previously, they stood in groups for their genital screenings), sterilized plastic speculums (previously, metal speculums were used repeatedly for each worker), disposable paper sheeting for examination beds, and more respectful treatment by doctors and staff in the clinic.

The members of Las Magdalenas encourage new arrivals on the street to register at the city clinic. As legal sex workers often in the public eye, they will not allow an illegal worker to obtain membership. This affords them the ability to encourage standardized practices and pricing among fellow legal street workers in the Coahuila district. In this neighborhood, those who work as illegals are treated with hostility and occasional physical aggression. Legal members have at their disposal a vocal and respected group to take civil or human rights infractions to the civic authorities. Illegal workers do not—as illegal workers, they risk arrest for organizing protests or for making their occupational activities known to police.

Changes in the enforcement of regulations continue to change with each municipal election. In the summer of 2002, a crackdown on massage parlors effectively eliminated the majority of small entrepreneurs in the city. Many of these smaller operations were owned and operated by females. Only those businesses that had been well established (and, some say, able to bribe officials) were allowed to stay in business. All of these owners were men with strong financial standing. The crackdown, while morally satisfying to some, effectively consolidated power in the hands of a few well-connected persons and was considered an abuse of power among the sex workers I stayed in contact with. The standardization and professionalization of the industry should not require the displacement of competitors. Rather, the city should work with these businesses in order to help them comply with city regulations within an appointed time frame.

An additional change has occurred. Owing to continual police violence and harassment, a number of transgender sex workers moved to the town of Tecate, about an hour from Tijuana. Local residents, outraged at the influx of a handful of transgendered sex workers, have pressured their own officials to crack down on the newcomers. In this case, a new town ordinance will criminalize cross-dressing and allow police to imprison men who wear women's clothes (BBC News 2002). Fears about AIDS pervade their arguments. The ordinance is one of many to have been passed throughout the state under the guise of good conduct. Because of threats by gay prostitutes that they would release the names of those soliciting them, the Tijuana council members promised not to invoke the ordinance. These kinds of ordinances serve to condone homophobic behavior and further stigmatize those who already suffer extreme social ostracism. Specific human and civil rights mandates are needed to protect both sex workers and persons with alternative sexualities. In the absence of these mandates, working conditions will continue to be determined by outsiders who care little about the impact of violence and stigma on the mental and physical health of already marginalized individuals.

The fluctuations in the policing of certain neighborhoods and businesses and fights over the right to work on certain streets reflect a tension between various sectors of the city and their use rights as residents of the city. By examining these processes, one can begin to understand the moral economy in which sex work takes place, and the way in which the social status and power of the governing group are reinforced and contested.[18] In the context of the sex industry in Tijuana, surveillance, especially targeted surveillance of specific places and particular subjects, whether by civil authorities, politicians, police, city clinics, media, or even researchers, does affect both the sense of community and the community-making process among stigmatized social groups. Because of the potential violence associated with their trade, community involvement could very well be a protective factor for sex workers in this city. Legal workers, who are protected by their legal status, have an easier time building a sense of community and interreliance. Familiarity not only builds a sense of community but is a very important strategy to reduce harm associated with occupational risks and dangerous neighborhoods. The policing of particular spaces through harassment, violence, jail time, and fines forces illegal sex workers to stay mobile in order to prevent encounters with the police. This, in turn, prevents them from gaining familiarity with places and people to rely on in times of need.

In this context, policing represents a health risk because of its potential violence, because of its impact on mental health and the experience of social stigma, and because it discourages community involvement, which may protect against customer violence. Improving the quality of life of sex workers will require placing their real needs over the city's politics.

CHAPTER SIX

Gender Diversity

The public's collective knowledge about sex work is largely formed by stereotypes of and research conducted on female street prostitutes, particularly drug-addicted prostitutes, who often have a difficult time negotiating transactions with customers, are frequently taken advantage of, and are generally viewed as being out of control as a result of their addictions. These representations are given added weight because they dovetail with fears about female sexuality gone out of control, moral decline, and social disorder. While this may not represent an entirely accurate picture of even a small proportion of sex workers, the stereotype pervades many representations of prostitution in the contemporary popular imagination. We know very little, however, about the everyday lives of sex workers, addicted or not, much less about how sex work might be experienced differently by men, women, and transgenders.

Among female sex workers, access to professional status increases both the sense of agency as well as actual control over the transaction. Noneffeminate male sex workers can utilize their role as *machos*, emphasizing their dominance and dangerousness, but because they do not have access to either professional or legal status and because they work in more dangerous settings they are less able to control their transactions with customers. Male and transgender sex workers, the majority of whom do not work legally, are therefore at higher risk for nearly all occupational hazards. While no female, male, or transgender worker is in complete control of the sexual transaction, all are afforded access to various resources based on their gender and sexuality. As we shall see, both attempt to make compromises with their customers on the basis of their self-interest and ability to minimize risk. This sense of agency is removed by customers in the case of violence and rape.

Gender-based differences are a significant factor in how work is experienced, the ways in which occupational risks are dealt with, and the kinds of risks that are generally faced. Sex workers' health and safety are shaped by the social disparities between female, male, and transgender sex workers, the role of gender in shaping their lives prior to sex work, the gendered nature of their experiences as sex workers, the level of agency they have in negotiating with their clients and the police, and the ways they differ in terms of relationships with their customers and work practices. Sex workers are able to exercise varying degrees of personal control in their transactions with clients through their decision to work in particular settings and refusal to service particular customers; they also exercise control in defining the terms of the sexual transaction, including the sexual acts to be performed, the use of condoms, price setting, and time limit. Because the degree of agency involved in one's work may differ according to one's gender and background, gender can be said to be a significant factor in health outcomes related to HIV/AIDS, stigma, violence, mental health, and drug addiction.

This chapter will illustrate how gender appears to work in defining occupational experiences as well as examine the linkages between gender and occupational health risks. Female, male, and transgender sex workers differ extensively, both in terms of their demographic backgrounds and as to their overall approach to work, work experiences, and occupational risks. Each faces specific challenges in relation to his or her gender both before and after entering sex work. In this section, I discuss the basic differences among the three groups and then move on to examine their work experiences and practices. Table 6.1 illustrates some of the demographic patterns found based on gender.

Transgender Sex Workers

Most commercial transgender[1] work sites are located in the periphery of the Coahuila district, along one street in particular. A few clubs have reputations for employing both female and transgender workers, but for the most part transgender workers face marginal opportunities for employment as compared with females. They are integrated into the regulated system: there are a few popular clubs which employ only transgender workers and are licensed to employ legal workers. In Tijuana, transgenders tend to make less than female sex workers in the upscale clubs but have earnings similar to those of female sex workers in established working- or middle-class type clubs. Transgender sex workers in this study, although they tended to be more highly educated than the majority of female sex workers, faced widespread discrimination in terms of finding other forms of employment because of their trans-

Table 6.1. Demographic Characteristics (by Gender) (percentages)

	Female	*Male*	*Trans*
Average age (Age range)	26(12–56) years	22(16–35) years	26(17–63) years
Can read Spanish	96	93	100
Can speak English	23	38	31
Noncommercial partner	60	36	25
Two or more noncommercial partners	5	10	6
Single/never married	50	69	81
Living with a partner	22	24	19
Separated from a spouse	9	5	0
Married	7	2	0
Widowed	0	0	0
Divorced	11	0	0
Have one or more children	81	19	0
Children are living with them	54	2	0

gender characteristics and sexual orientation. As suggested by Weinberg et al. (1999), transgender workers hold a unique appeal for their customers because of their ability to combine a feminine gendered performance with male sexual characteristics.

The relative acceptance of the commercial relationship between transgendered workers and their customers may further indicate the importance of gender (rather than actual sexual activity) in defining acceptable commercial sex work in the Latin American context. Those who pass as female are generally treated like other female sex workers in terms of surveillance; health inspectors and the police work to get them registered and prevent them from working illegally. Their social role as female prostitutes appears to supersede their biological origins.

Male Sex Workers

Work venues for male sex workers tend to overlap the general contours of urban gay life in Tijuana; the majority work in or near cruising sites, gay clubs, and saunas. A few work in massage parlors with female or transgender workers or both. They are primarily targeted by the police for their street activities, which may involve petty crime, loitering, drug use or drug dealing, and so on. They are not targeted by health inspectors for registration purposes, and they are not encouraged to register as sex workers. Their commercial activities are largely ignored by the civic authorities.

Mexico is largely a conservative, Catholic country whose population exhibits widespread homophobia. It is unlikely that male–male sexual transactions, commercial or otherwise, would be accepted by the general public or condoned by health officials. The entire world of male–male sexual transactions is rarely acknowledged in Tijuana, perhaps because it involves men, who benefit from a greater level of tolerance and entitlement with respect to their private sexual behavior. In much of the world, men are rarely targeted by public health or law enforcement officials as either customers or workers. While sexual transactions by females are often treated as public (and dangerous) in nature, those involving men are not. Although the disregard shown toward male sexual behavior is a form of social privilege that might appear to benefit individual males, it ultimately prevents a sense of shared responsibility for reproductive and sexual health.

Comparing Gender-Based Differences

The majority of the participants in the three groups I interviewed for this book were in their twenties, but the average age of male sex workers was lower (twenty-two) compared to that of females (twenty-six) and transgenders (twenty-six). The youngest participant was a female sex worker aged twelve, and the eldest was a transgender sex worker who was sixty-three. Special considerations for youth sex workers, who are unable to register or work in any upscale establishment legally, are discussed in a following section. That men were more likely to speak English (38 percent) than either transgenders (31 percent) or females (23 percent) reflects their greater interaction with U.S. customers in commercial sex work and other industries as well as their greater exposure to working, traveling, and living in the United States.

Females were most likely to have a regular sexual partner (60 percent) and the least likely to have multiple regular sexual partners (only 5 percent), but 19 to 24 percent of the total number of members in the three groups were living with their regular sexual partner at the time of the study. Transgenders were more likely than either group to be single and living alone (81 percent)—none had been married, divorced, separated, or widowed.

Sex workers of every age are not just sex workers—they are also daughters, sons, mothers, fathers, sisters, and brothers with very real economic responsibilities that may encourage them to practice commercial sex work.[2] In fact, family obligations to parents and other relatives left behind in sending communities as well as to children under their care and planned investments in the home community—for example, building a house for themselves, parents, and children, alternate businesses, school costs for younger siblings, children, and often nieces and nephews—are the most common reasons for entry into sex work as well as the most significant regular expenses, other than personal living expenses, for the majority of the sex workers I spoke with. Sex work is a strategy that allows marginalized people to earn more money than they would be able to otherwise.

Female sex workers were more likely to have children than male or transgender workers (81 compared to 19 percent and 0 percent, respectively) and to have them living under their care (54 percent compared to 2 percent and 0 percent) rather than with parents or a former partner. This finding illustrates the importance of the mother's role in caring for children, but it also indicates the potential importance of remaining secretive about sex work activities and maintaining boundaries between work and nonwork activities. It also contributes substantially to the stress and anxiety involved in keeping one's work activities a secret. Females are much more likely to support their child dependents and demonstrate a higher level of need with respect to earning goals and longer work hours. None of the transgendered workers had children, and many may have been sterile owing to hormone use. Although one in five male sex workers had children, only 2 percent were living under their care.

Social Networks

Many sex workers in Tijuana are tightly integrated into family networks extending into other areas of Mexico. Migratory work is an integral factor in the subsistence strategies of the majority of families in Mexico, often taking the form of agricultural work throughout California, Florida, and the Midwest. Sex workers also follow these migratory networks, traveling to catchment areas like Tijuana or venturing into agricultural areas in the United States on a seasonal, rotating basis. Sex work migration appears to function in much the same way as other forms of migration. All of the participants in this study discussed the role of sex work activities in relation to seasonal work routes, extensive regional social networks, and economic support in the form of remittances.[3] Table 6.2 illustrates the gendered distribution of social networks and migration practices. Family ties and responsibilities figured prominently in the lives of these sex workers. Up to 50 percent provide the primary income needed to help build the family home, to send siblings to school, or to buy food and medical care for aging parents. Forty-one to forty-five percent visit

Table 6.2. Social Networks and Migration (by Gender) (percentages)

	Female	Male	Trans
Visit family home regularly	41	45	44
Live with family part of the year	41	29	31
Plan to return permanently	19	21	31
Earn money while visiting family home	9	31	31
. . . as sex workers	<1%	7	13
Regularly send parents/siblings money	31	21	50
Pay for parents'/siblings' living costs	6	17	38
Pay for family business	2	2	6
Pay for family home	1	0	6
Regularly cross to United States	42	64	63
. . . in order to work	11	31	19
. . . in order to visit family	13	10	6
. . . in order to have fun	18	24	38

family in other areas of Mexico regularly every year, 29 percent–41 percent live with those family members, usually parents and siblings, while they are there, and many (19 to 31 percent) plan to return home someday. Few were involved in the wage labor market while at home, choosing to spend their time reconnecting with their friends and loved ones, especially their children.

Females especially are involved in a seasonal form of migration—31 percent send regular monetary support to family members in other parts of the country, in addition to providing for the family members who live with them in Tijuana. Male remittances deriving from sex work activities are the lowest of the three groups. This may be the case either because male sex workers are more likely to be permanent residents, living on their own without children to care for, or because they don't earn enough to send remittances. More work in this area needs to be done.

Transgender workers were also heavily involved in the support of their family members in sending communities (even more so than females)—over 50 percent sent money home regularly. It may be that although transgender workers did not have children to support and thus did not adopt a mothering role, their gender performance does include the acquisition of the role of dutiful daughter or sister, which would encourage this support. Their lack of child dependents may allow them to exploit this role more fully than females. Further interviews would need to be conducted to confirm this point.

Contrary to what I expected, permanent migration to the United States was not a priority for these participants. One participant did indicate that s/he wanted to work in San Francisco as a "drag queen," while a few others indicated that they enjoyed traveling in the United States or making money there but didn't want to live there permanently. Many had the opportunity to stay in the United States (42 to 63 percent migrated back and forth from the United States in order to work but also to visit family, have fun, shop, and travel), but most returned from the United States willingly and preferred living in Mexico, their cultural homeland, among their family and friends. A few wanted to stay in the United States but were deported because they didn't have the necessary documentation to stay legally. The majority pre-ferred Mexico, saying that they were treated poorly in the United States and that they had experienced too many linguistic or cultural barriers and dis-crimination. Many felt that the greater emphasis on family and social relations in Mexico was more appealing.

Even so, only one of out five planned to return home (that is, to a city other than Tijuana) permanently. This may indicate one of two feelings: a growing preference for a newfound standard of living in the city and a new life or identity apart from one's family and potentially more conservative home community; or fear that they will be ostracized by members in the sending community for their sex work activities in Tijuana.

Social and Economic Vulnerability

Levels of vulnerability, access to social supports, and the nature of those social supports varied by gender. The variation reflects the more general organiza-tion of gender relations in Latin America, where family and intimate part-ner relations are more significant to female support networks, and same-sex peer networks are more significant resources to males. These differences are illustrated in table 6.3. Of the three groups, male sex workers were the most vulnerable socially and economically and the most likely to become involved in a variety of criminal activities. They were also the most likely to have en-gaged in commercial sex work at a younger age than either of the other groups. Whereas women were more deeply enmeshed in family responsibilities and caretaking, male sex workers were the most likely to be out on their own with-out sufficient social supports. Although support from family members was low among all three groups, economic dependence on regular sexual partners was important to one out of three females but was nonexistent among males and transgenders. Instead, males and transgenders were much more likely to rely on friends for additional support in time of need (26 percent and 13 percent

Table 6.3. Signs of Vulnerability (by Gender) (percentages)

	Female	Male	Trans
Currently homeless	1	7	6
Living in rehabilitation	0	2	0
No safe place to stay (past three years)	23	67	44
Incarcerated	23	62	63
Has another job	31	57	38
Smuggles immigrants, steals, sells drugs	2	7	0
Economic support from their family	6	10	13
Economic support from a sexual partner	27	0	0
Economic support from their friends	2	26	13
Age at first commercial sex transaction	22 years	17 years	19 years
Age range for first transaction	12–41 years	7–24 years	7–63 years

respectively), whereas only 2 percent of females relied on peers for economic support. Transgender sex workers appear to model both males and females in that they relied on their peer networks (13 percent) as often as they relied on their families (13 percent).

Sexual Orientation

In his work with street kids on the U.S.–Mexico border, Taylor (2001) concludes that in Mexico, "where you are from" is far more important than "what you do." This can be easily applied to sex work in terms of the difference between personal sexual orientation and actual customer base. Sex workers can keep their personal sexual identity intact, while still engaging in a variety of sexual activities as part of a commercial exchange. In particular, male sex workers may engage in a form of *functional bisexuality* which allows men to have sex with other men without necessarily identifying themselves as homosexual or even bisexual.[4]

The role of sexual orientation in shaping the kinds of customers that are seen as desirable and acceptable appears to differ by gender. As table 6.4 illustrates, work activities may not be a significant factor in defining sexual orientation and identity among men. While the majority of female sex workers identified as heterosexual (96 percent) and had only male customers (93 percent), male sex workers were much more diverse in terms of sexual orientation and clientele. For women, the sex/gender of the customer correlated with sexual orientation, although there were some exceptions. Prior to the survey portion of this study, I did have an informal conversation with a self-identified lesbian who stated that she accepted only male customers, out of respect for her primary relationship. However, none of the survey participants self-identified as lesbian; and only one female did not accept male partners. A few females self-identified as bisexual (4 percent), and accepted both male and female customers (4 percent). No females stated that they were uncertain of their sexual orientation. Bisexual males and self-identified gay men were much easier to find; few male sex workers (12 percent) and no transgender sex workers identified as heterosexual. Although many transgender individuals in the United States may identify as heterosexual (for example, a male to female transgender who desires only male partners does not necessarily see herself as gay), all of the transgender sex workers in this study self-identified as gay (81 percent) or bisexual (13 percent). Only 6 percent of transgender workers were uncertain of their sexual orientation. Male sex workers were more likely than female or transgender workers to be unsure of their sexual orientation (17 percent), to self-identify as bisexual (33 percent) or gay (38 percent), and to have customers that were male, female, or transgender (21 percent). Only 7 percent of male sex workers limited their sex work transactions to females.

These findings raise questions about the impact of sexual orientation on customer selection and, specifically, about the role sexuality plays in commercial sex. Although the sexual aspects of sex work are often downplayed by sex workers, sexuality may play a role in the comfort level of certain types of sex work activities. This is clearly a relationship that needs to be explored further.

Table 6.4. Sexual Partners (by Gender) (percentages)

	Female	Male	Trans
Sexual Orientation/Identity:			
Bisexual	4	33	13
Gay	0	38	81
Heterosexual	96	12	0
Questioning	0	17	6
Gender Background of Customers:			
Only male customers	93	36	69
Only female customers	1	7	0
Male and female customers	4	36	31
Male, female, and transgender customers	<1	21	0

Solicitation and Transaction Sites

The greater sexual flexibility experienced by male sex workers is also reflected in solicitation sites and locations for sexual transactions. Nearly all of the female sex workers worked in bars, nightclubs, massage parlors, and the street areas in front of these establishments. A handful worked through word-of-mouth from friends who acted as contacts for potential customers. This can be contrasted by the greater diversity of solicitation sites for male and transgender workers, as illustrated in table 6.5. Bars and nightclubs are still important solicitation sites for male and transgender sex workers, as are the street areas in front of them, but other outdoor and indoor sites are also used. The Plaza Sta. Cecilia, a community shopping area by day and gay mecca by night, was used by 64 percent of the male sex workers—but by none of the transgender workers. At night, the plaza is a dangerous, male-oriented place which sees few females, including male-to-female transgenders. An assortment of other outdoor sites, parks, and cafés served as meeting places for male sex workers and their customers. Some used their own homes or the homes of friends to meet their customers, while others relied on Internet chatrooms, parties, saunas, or bathrooms to solicit. Their greater chances for physical mobility and flexibility reflect gender norms and the social use of space in Mexico.

The movements of female sex workers (and women more generally) are highly curtailed, especially at night. Gender ideologies about women and the dangers found outside the home and about women outside the protection of males encourage females to work inside the home or to at least stay indoors, especially at night. Females out on their own at night are targets—and they are viewed with suspicion as potential sex workers, whereas males are not. Violence toward females, whether threatened or actual, and rape of females as well as police surveillance and harassment reinforce the perceived need of this "protected" status. Transgender workers, who recognize these gender norms, are also relegated to particular spaces at particular times of the day or evening. Interestingly, transgender workers were also very likely to rely on phone or taxi referrals to solicit customers, presumably because of the unique nature of their services or their fear of violence or both. Male sex workers, on the other hand, are able to cloak their solicitation practices in an atmosphere of male pleasure and recreation.

As I illustrate in table 6.6, the preferred locations for sexual transactions also reflect the greater degree of mobility among male sex workers and the greater rigidity of sex work among females, who engage in more standardized transactions. While all sex workers use hotel rooms rented specifically for the transaction (under the watchful eye of staff), most female sex workers use

Table 6.5. Solicitation Sites (by Gender) (percentages)

	Female	Male	Trans
Street	22	67	94
Bar/disco	22	67	81
Massage parlor	76	7	19
Plaza Sta. Cecilia	0	64	0
Friends/word of mouth	13	45	31
Park	0	38	13
Home/neighborhood	3	31	6
Parties	4	24	31
Sauna/bathhouse	0	17	0
Internet chat room	<1	10	13
Bathroom	0	10	0
Café	1	10	19
Advertisement	<1	5	0
Shopping center	0	0	6
Phone/call service	<1	0	13
Taxi driver	0	0	13

Note: Respondents were not required to select the most frequent solicitation site. They were allowed to include all sites they used on a regular basis.

hotels physically connected to their solicitation site. Male sex workers are far more likely to use a customer's room or home (86 percent), which involves a greater degree of risk because they are the most private and most difficult to control. Women were the least likely to engage in sexual transactions outdoors (only 5 percent as compared with 36 percent of males and 75 percent of transgenders). Alleys or abandoned buildings were the venues most commonly used by both males (26 percent) and transgenders (50 percent). Transgenders were the only group to rely extensively on their own homes (56 percent) or friends' homes (31 percent) to entertain customers. Their sex work activities were more closely linked to their personal lifestyle and activities with casual partners.

Female and male sex workers were more likely than transgender sex workers to keep their sex work activities a secret from their friends, neighbors, and families. Although 12 percent of males used their homes, they were able to portray their relationships as homosocial friendships without risk of stigma. Only 1 percent of female workers used their own homes for this purpose. Their sexual activities and relationships are more susceptible to exposure, gossip, and ostracism.

Table 6.6. Place of Sexual Transaction (by Gender) (percentages)

	Female	Male	Trans
Nearby hotel	100	100	100
Customer's room	30	86	69
Customer's car	8	45	69
Friend's home	3	24	31
Their own home	1	12	56
Outdoor location	5	36	75
. . . Alley	2	26	50
. . . Stairway	1	21	13
. . . Restroom	1	5	6

Note: Respondents were not required to select the most frequent place of sexual transaction. They were allowed to include all sites they used on a regular basis.

Nonmonetary Sexual Exchange

Nonmonetary sexual exchange can indicate not only a greater level of vulnerability, but also something about the gendered nature of sexual exchange. In the context of extensive poverty, noncommercial sexual exchanges in the form of food, shelter, clothing, and so on are defined as "survival sex" (Farmer et al. 1996). In many ways, these exchanges resemble the romantic entanglements associated with sex among noncommercial partners. In my neighborhood, older gay men and younger male sex workers sought out these kinds of relationships for their mutual benefit.

The nature and greater prevalence of nonmonetary commercial sexual exchange among male and some transgender sex workers seem to indicate that such males relied on customer relations to bring about such exchanges because of a lack of other forms of social support; that commercial transactions among these male sex workers are more flexible in that a fair exchange value is determined at the point of sale rather than on standard market value; that commercial relations among males sometimes cross over into their nonwork social worlds; and that transgender workers are more like males than females in terms of the flexibility of their exchanges with customers. My findings, which are illustrated in table 6.7, appear to support these conclusions. These findings also illustrate that female sex work is more formal, institutionalized, and rigid in the framework of regulated sex work found in Tijuana. Informal sexual networking is nevertheless done by females, but it is less likely that this form of sexual exchange is seen as sex work per se—and it is carried out in the form of boyfriends or other casual relationships. Of course, regular clientele also provide additional gifts as signs of affection within a longer-term commercial transaction, but money is still an expected part of the transaction. From a customer's standpoint, these gifts are sometimes given in the hope that the relationship will transform into one that is more romantic and less commercial in nature. From the sex worker's standpoint, the gifts are tips for a job well done.

Social Relations with Customers

The greater informality of relationships between male and transgender sex workers and their customers is also reflected through higher levels of socialization with customers outside the immediate sexual transaction. Again, the distinction between work life and social life appears to be blurred more among male and transgender workers than among females. This may be related to the average number of customer transactions per week, which is lower among males and transgenders than among females. Because of differences in their lifestyles, male and transgender sex workers may take more time to develop customer relations, turning them into more casual friendship-like arrangements. For many female sex workers, these types of relationships seemed too much like courtship to make them comfortable. Many relied on the strict separation of their professional and private lives for psychological reasons or because they found their relationships with customers to be purely utilitarian and often disgusting or wanted to protect their children, family, or personal relations from knowing about these activities. These variations have not been adequately addressed theoretically but point toward the need for additional research in this area.

Table 6.7. Nonmonetary Sexual Exchange (by Gender) (percentages)

	Female	Male	Trans
Sex for food	3	21	38
Sex for shelter	1	5	6
Sex for clothes	9	36	31
Sex for luxury goods/gifts	9	38	31

Table 6.8. Social Relations with Customers (by Gender) (percentages)

	Female	Male	Trans
Average number of customers per week	N=8	N=2	N=5
Good friends with some customers	65	83	81
Customers visit them socially at home	24	67	44
Pay social visits to customer's home	8	26	75
Attend social events with customers	16	62	38
Have fallen in love with a customer	21	36	44
Have romantic feelings for customers	30	57	56

Socialization with customers takes many forms, as is illustrated in table 6.8. Male and transgender workers were more likely to be on friendly terms with regular customers, visiting them at home, being visited by them in their own home, or attending social events. Both were more likely than females to have developed romantic feelings toward their customers or to have fallen in love. The prevalence of romantic attachments between customers and sex workers in this study was surprising, especially considering that the narratives describe the stressful psychological nature of commercial sex. Transgender workers were more likely than males or females to pay social visits and form romantic attachments. Again, this may indicate that in this context at least, the social lines between customers and lovers or friends are blurred more in the case of male and transgender workers than they are for females, and even more so for transgenders. Lifestyle and sociability are more tightly integrated into their work lives than in those of females, who often have families and lives very separate from their work downtown. These divergences indicate, first, that social norms and acceptable sexual behavior are quite different for females than for males and transgenders and, second, that achieving sexual respectability at home and among neighbors is important to many female sex workers in spite of their occupation.

Gender-Based Sexual Risk

HIV/AIDS rates among sex workers do not help one understand the nature of occupational risk in Tijuana. Far more prevalent are occupational hazards in the form of violence, mental health problems, and drug and alcohol addiction—all of which are highly gendered. However, each of these hazards can also increase the likelihood of exposure to HIV. In addition, the devastation caused by AIDS makes this a very relevant issue, one that needs to be addressed. Among the participants in this study, 19 percent of transgender sex workers were infected with HIV/AIDS, whereas 5 percent of male and 4 percent of female sex workers were infected. Because most workers reported widespread condom use with their customers, the variation may indicate that HIV risk among transgender workers is more likely related to risk practices while not at work or risk practices that are not sexual in nature. Or it may reflect inaccuracies in reporting condom use. By contextualizing the numerical data within a more qualitative understanding of sexual risk in this setting, we will see that the greater likelihood of exposure and infection among transgender sex workers is not necessarily a result of their work per se but arises out of a complex combination of anatomical (anal sex without condoms is more likely to lead to infection than vaginal sex without condoms) and social differences.

Sexual Risk with Noncommercial Partners

In noncommercial sexual relationships, transgender workers were the most likely to have engaged in sex with a partner who they knew was HIV-positive (31 percent), an intravenous drug user (38 percent), or bisexual or gay (100 percent) (see table 6.9). Because anal receptive intercourse characterizes the majority of the sexual interactions among transgenders, it is highly likely

Table 6.9. Sexual Risk Practices (by Gender) (percentages)

	Female	Male	Trans
No condom used (last customer)	1	19	44
Condom breakage (past month)	34	24	56
Always place the condom	79	53	63
Water-based lubricant	41	36	56
Oil-based lubricant	2	12	13
Unknown lubricant	4	14	0
No lubricant	50	71	81
Sexually Transmitted Infections:			
STI checkup	58	43	50
STI symptoms (past six months)	19	21	6
STI treatment	100	67	0

that the level of HIV infection among transgender sex workers is related to this practice in their personal lives. Sex with known positive partners was extremely low among females (<1 percent) and among males (7 percent). Sex with intravenous drug-using partners was higher, about 16 percent among females and 24 percent among males. Sex with bisexual or gay partners was the most frequent activity in terms of added risk, 39 percent among females and 81 percent among males. Noncommercial sexual relationships represent potential sources of infection for all sex workers, just as they do for workers involved in other occupations. Receiving semen into the vagina or anus greatly increases risk for females, transgenders, and men who have sex with men. Condom use to prevent sexual infection, however, remains low, even among those who understand HIV prevention techniques and have condoms available. The reasons for this have been well studied, especially with respect to women.[5] Some of these factors are gender specific, such as the desire to bear a child[6] and the inaccessibility of female-controlled prevention technology.

Others can be applied to all sex workers in this study. These factors include:

1. the desire to maintain stable relationships with husbands or lovers who may be infected or at-risk for becoming infected through another sexual partner;
2. the need to maintain liaisons with clients, boyfriends, and/or husbands for economic purposes;
3. the need to supply sex as a condition of employment, to supplement earnings with sex work, or to rely upon sex work for survival;
4. the lack of control over frequency of intercourse;
5. the danger of rape and other forms of sexual violence;
6. the denial of equal access to housing, education, legal protection, inheritance, employment, health care, and food.

Although these factors are discussed more frequently in terms of heightened female risk and pervasive gender inequities, they are relevant to all of the participants in this study. These particular workers were more vulnerable than males who were economically stable and not engaged in sex work, and more vulnerable than males who did not subvert gender and sexual norms.

Many of the sex workers in this study were more likely to be exposed to sexually transmitted infections through their romantic partners than through their customers—rates of condom use are much lower at home than at work (30 percent–40 percent vs. 90 percent–100 percent). Their romantic partnerships were treated in much the same way as romantic partnerships among other kinds of workers, in which condoms are simply not the norm.[7] Several of these participants suggested that their romantic partners were less likely to tolerate condom use than customers, who see condoms as a sexual norm in commercial transactions. Others expressed the belief that romantic partners were more loyal and trustworthy and therefore less likely to be infectious. *Not* using condoms was a marker of intimacy which differentiated between work sex and romantic attachments. This indicates a perception that while all sexual relationships carry some level of risk, sex workers perceive work sex as "riskier" than intimate partner sex in terms of potential infection. Those who did use condoms in their private relationships stated that they did so primarily to prevent unwanted pregnancy, but also because they wanted to protect both their partners and themselves from possible infection.

Sexual Risk with Customers

While condom use with customers is much higher than condom use with regular sexual partners, it does vary considerably by gender (see table 6.9). As discussed previously, registration status among females increases health-promoting behaviors and decreases sexual risk behavior in commercial transactions. Because transgender workers were less likely to work legally, and no males at the time of this study worked legally, these benefits remain highly gendered.

Females were the most likely to use condoms consistently with all their customers and to take charge of condom placement, and they were the least likely to use oil-based lubricants with latex condoms. Their vaginal secretions may have made it less necessary to use lubricant as often as male and transgender workers. Last, females were more likely than either group to receive regular STI checkups and to receive clinical treatment for STIs when necessary.

Accounts by customers appear to contradict these findings. When I shared some initial findings with customers, they indicated that condomless sex with Tijuana sex workers was far more prevalent than my findings illustrate. Their discussion forums include expansive discussions about how to get a sex worker to have sex without a condom, and their trip reports include stories about "barebacking," that is, having sex without a condom. Both sides have reason to exaggerate their condom use patterns: sex workers in order to protect their professional reputation, and customers to demonstrate their skill at manipulation and brag about their exploits. Self-narration is an important aspect of identity formation, as many anthropologists have demonstrated in work on various topics. Obtaining reliable self-reports regarding condom use is problematic. Ichikawa (1999) resorted to collecting condoms in order to avoid this obstacle. Albert (2001) used a combination of "complete observation" to collect empirical data firsthand, condom collection, and condom diaries. In designing this research study, I was not prepared for these contradictions and didn't realize the potential impact of integrating such innovative methods.

Transgender workers were the least likely of the three groups to practice consistent condom use with their customers. Condom breakage rates were also much higher among transgender workers, as was the use of oil-based lubricants with latex condoms. Transgender workers were the least likely to engage in safer sexual techniques with customers, or to do so successfully. This represents a definite health risk for them as well as for their customers.

For all three groups, when condoms were not used with customers it was because they were familiar with them, they trusted them, they believed them to have a low risk of infection (usually because the customer was married), they didn't like using condoms, there wasn't a condom available, they wanted the customer to finish more quickly, or they were paid extra to have sex without a condom. All were aware of the protective benefits of condoms as protection against STI and HIV/AIDS.

Gender Ideology and Social Status

Sex workers are able to exercise varying degrees of personal control in their transactions with clients through their decision to work in particular settings and refusal to service particular customers; they also exercise control in defining the terms of the sexual transaction, including the sexual acts to be performed, the use of condoms, price setting, and time limit. Culturally informed understandings of gender among both sex workers and their customers provide a toolbox of potential resources useful in weighing the transaction in favor of one particular party. Neither is in complete control of the transaction. Each is afforded access to different social and cultural resources to protect her or his self-interests. The transaction process is, above all, a negotiation in which neither party is either all-powerful or completely powerless.

Among female sex workers, appeals to professional status or to the sympathies of customers can increase both the sense of agency as well as actual control over the transaction. In extended transactions, relative power in the transaction can be enhanced in favor of the worker through personal narratives which play on the sensitivities and values of particular customers. In this study, the participants could weigh the transaction in their favor by indicating the following: sexual inexperience and naiveté (being new to the job or being new to a particular sexual act); victimization and vulnerability; rural background and traditional family values; romantic interest and emotional attachment; visible sexual attraction; in the case of female workers, dutiful motherhood (*marianismo*) and the need to support family dependents; and, in the case of male workers, sexual dominance, masculinity (being macho), and threat of danger and retaliation.

In Mexico, the culturally based ideology of marianismo, which includes strong assumptions about and expectations for female sexual innocence and purity and dutiful motherhood, offers culturally based tools useful in customer transactions.[8] However, the idealization of "true womanhood" also lays the groundwork for the social stigma faced by female sex workers, who subvert this gender role by their sexual activities. It is precisely this social stigma that puts sex workers at elevated risk for violence, mental illness, drug addiction, and HIV/AIDS.

Goldstein (1994), for example, argues that marianismo complicates risk reduction among Latinas in that they may be less likely, less willing, and less able to negotiate safer sex practices with their male partners. In Latin America, cultural attitudes toward female sexuality, especially distinctions between "decent" and "indecent" women, can make it difficult for women to openly discuss sexuality or negotiate sexual behavior. In noncommercial transactions, condom use denotes acceptance or suspicion of a partner's infidelity or infection.

In commercial transactions, female sex workers subvert the sexual aspects of this ideology through their greater sexual experience and activities with multiple sexual partners. Within this constraint, they can either downplay their sexual experience or emphasize the development of professional practices, such as consistent condom use. Appeals to professionalism allow them to openly negotiate their sexual boundaries, use condoms, and engage in erotic transgressive acts with customers without appearing to be out of control. A certain level of respectability and self-esteem is found through the development of professional work practices, which include both personal narratives shared with customers and the discipline of physical hygiene, regular medical exams, and consistent condom use. The professionalism of (some) workers in Tijuana was found to be very appealing to the customers I interviewed. Thus, while stigmatized in terms of public opinion because of their sexual behavior, the specific ways in which they controlled that behavior afforded them a level of respectability, at least within the work venue.

Similar to fears of female sexuality spiraling out of control are fears that the poor represent a class that is out of control. Because the majority of sex workers in Tijuana come from working-class or underclass backgrounds, their greater access to wealth as a result of their work affords them a higher level of class status and therefore respectability than they would have had otherwise. Poverty carries its own stigma—a burden that may be more difficult to carry than that of falling short of gendered sexual ideals. Identifying with and living as a high-class sex worker, was more appealing and glamorous for many of my participants than living as a person who is thought of as lazy, dirty, or stupid and who has no chance of improving herself through class mobility. Eventually, they stated, they will move to another place or return home and create a new identity divorced from their sexual past.

In Mexico (as in the United States), male promiscuity offers more social rewards than social stigma. Within this gendered system, sexual conquest and sexual experience are idealized as part of machismo—or what it means to be a man. Male sex workers, while they face social stigma for their sexual relations with men, are not stigmatized for having multiple sexual partners in the form of customers. Their ability to exploit customers for pay or pleasure forms a part of their claims for respect and status among their peers, especially on the street. Commercial sexual relations with women, especially foreign women from wealthy countries, are discussed with a mixture of humor and conceit.

Male sex workers who have sex with male customers do face varying degrees of stigma depending on the nature of their gendered performance and sexual relations. Thus, an effeminate male (*maricón*) subverts gender norms associated with masculinity and therefore faces social stigma in a way that aggressive, macho workers do not. Receptive anal sex is also highly stigmatized, as it is associated with female passivity, whereas active anal sex is less so.

Transgender sex workers subvert and challenge gender and sexual norms in a way that female and male sex workers do not. While attractive to some customers because of their unique characteristics, they can face widespread abuse and harassment because of their transgendered status by those outside of their immediate social world. Misunderstood, feared, and held in contempt, transgender sex workers face social stigma first according to their gender status and only secondarily to their status as men who have sex with men, or sex workers. Unlike male sex workers, who characterize some of their sexual relationships with male customers as macho, transgender sex workers are denigrated as homosexuals regardless of their sexual behavior. Their greater susceptibility to social stigma based on their gendered and sexual status increases their exposure to occupational violence, drug addiction, and HIV/AIDS.

Table 6.10. Occupational Violence Experienced (by Gender) (percentages)

	Female	Male	Trans
Perpetrator:			
Customer	27	24	56
Manager/Employer	<1	2	6
Police	6	21	63
Stranger	7	19	38
Types of Violence:			
Threats	17	36	44
Slap/kick	9	14	44
Robbed	9	19	56
Kidnapped	4	7	13
Raped	20	17	56
Strangulation/attempted murder	7	2	13
Violence reported	5	7	25

Gender, Violence, and Mental Health

Particular settings and types of stigma may encourage certain forms of violence. Thus, the relationship between gender and the sexual geography of the sex industry is particularly important in structuring occupational risk. As is illustrated in table 6.10, exposure to certain forms of occupational violence varies considerably by gender and in very diverse ways. In this study, male workers were slightly less susceptible to customer violence, presumably because of the perception among customers that they might retaliate. However, because they commonly worked in areas widely regarded as the most dangerous, crime-ridden areas of the city, they were far more likely to be exposed to police violence and violence associated with petty theft. While less likely than either group to be raped, strangled, or knifed, they were twice as likely to be threatened, slapped, kicked, punched, robbed, or kidnapped. Among both males and females, very few of these incidents were ever reported.

As table 6.10 illustrates, transgender sex workers faced the highest rates of all forms of violence surveyed. They were twice as likely to face customer violence, three to six times more likely to face violence at the hands of employers, three to ten times more likely to encounter police violence, and two to four times more likely to be accosted by strangers. Rape and robbery were experienced more than any other form of violence. Clearly, violence is a serious health risk for this segment of the population.

Table 6.11. Stress and Depressive Symptoms (by Gender) (percentages)

	Female	Male	Trans
Average number of symptoms (ten-point scale)	N=6	N=5	N=5
Felt symptoms were connected to work	77	64	63
Types of Symptoms:			
Sadness	74	52	63
Loss of interest/pleasure	43	38	50
Change in appetite	64	45	56
Change in sleeping patterns	61	43	56
Anxiety	51	31	25
Loss of energy	50	38	56
Feelings of shame/guilt	77	71	63
Inability to concentrate	54	52	31
Loss of libido	48	29	44
Suicidal thoughts	21	26	38

I have never worked at something like this and I feel the dirtiest of women. It makes me feel very filthy. Every time I get home I am ashamed because I feel that everyone sees me. That everybody points at me. I do not feel normal. I do not want to talk to anyone. I want to be alone. Sometimes I feel desperate and want to run out of there. (Leticia, twenty-six, female sex worker)

Pervasive violence and social stigma translated into higher-than-average rates of stress and depressive symptoms among all sex workers in this study. The experience of mental stress can be highly gendered, based on feelings of shame, guilt, and stigma associated with the subversion of gender and sexual ideals. Table 6.11 illustrates my findings, which are based on a ten-point scale for common symptoms of depression, but the narratives I will share are far more telling. All three groups experienced extremely high rates of what would be diagnosed as chronic depression, that is, at least three or more of the symptoms for a period of several weeks. Females experienced more depressive symptoms than either males or transgenders. Male workers fell in between both groups in the prevalence of each of these symptoms but were less able to articulate their feelings in relation to their work. The majority of all workers have coped with these symptoms anywhere from a few months to several years. The vast majority felt that their symptoms were directly connected to their work.

Even more than transgenders, females were likely to describe feelings of sadness, shame, anxiety, and a loss of appetite, sleep, and libido—a loss of self-esteem directly related to their loss of sexual agency at work:

> You feel sort of dirty when you are in this, ashamed. You lose confidence in yourself also. You feel like everybody is looking at you when you leave [from work], that they are all pointing at you. . . . I feel shame, I feel dirty. Confused sometimes. That I do not love myself, because if I loved myself, I would take better care. In not having sex for money. I no longer go with the persons that did not want to use a condom. (Elvira, twenty, female sex worker)

Feelings of stigma-related shame make female sex workers extremely reluctant to disclose their work status to intimate friends and family, and they attempt to keep their work lives separate from their family lives as much as possible. Although female sex workers attempted to separate their work lives from their personal lives, the added stress involved in sex work often permeated that boundary:

> My work makes me have feelings of shame. Until now I have had the capacity to separate it [from home]. In my job I work. My house is something very much apart from what I do. (Ana, twenty-seven, female sex worker)

The vast majority of female workers expressed particularly strong negative feelings associated with social stigma, fear of rejection, having to lie to loved ones, or not being able to be a good role model for their children. Many expressed fear of rejection and violent reprisal at the hands of family members and regular sexual partners:

> It has affected me emotionally, in making decisions, my family sometimes. I feel dirty, guilty for this, for what I am doing. My partner also. He will kill me if he finds out I work at this. He would throw me in the trash. I need help to remove myself from this, from what I am living. I have hidden what I do from my family for a long time. If they found out I would commit suicide. (Micaela, twenty-four, female sex worker)

Feeling forced into sex work because of economic circumstances and desperation greatly elevates feelings of anger and depression, sometimes increasing the likelihood of drug use:

Sometimes I do not feel like working and I feel forced to work, and a client calls me [on the phone] and it is the person I am least comfortable with. I feel very forced. I am tolerating persons that mean nothing to me, being with other bodies is not what I am about. I get mad after that, I feel that I am forced to have relations for money even though I do not like the person and that makes me mad. When I am with a client I think that I am not doing it because I want to, but because of need, having to stand someone. Or getting yourself all drugged so he feels that I do a good job. (Hacinta, female sex worker)

In some ways, this is connected to feelings of disgust toward customers:

In reality I do not like the job. It is disgusting because you have contact with many men and they leer at you with lust and evil. For me, being with one client after another is disgusting. No matter how long I may have been in this, I cannot get accustomed. All this depresses you. Depression sets in. (Leah, thirty-two, female sex worker)

In others, the emotional distress related to sex work results from the physical and mental exhaustion that sets in as a result of repetitive sexual activity and the effect of that exhaustion in limiting their ability to be sexual with their regular partner:

Because of the abuse of sex work, I feel fatigued, my back aches, I feel that sex work tires me out. Imagine. So much being with one and with another and another. By the time you want to be with your partner, you do not even get the urge. Sometimes I get home tired and I have to get there to bathe, to take away the smell of cigarettes, because my daughter hugs me and I have to sleep with her at night. (Zapopa, thirty-one, female sex worker)

[This work] affects me in three ways. [First], I get tired because the mister is fucking and fucking and he does not end and I get tired. Second, if they smell bad I get nauseous and third, after fucking so much I want nothing with my partner. (Ofelia, forty-one, female sex worker)

In contrast, some transgender sex workers expressed occasional enhancement of self-esteem in relation to their work activities:

It makes me feel, on the one hand, that I do it well, I like to be told [as much]. But I wish I could be useful for something else, if I have some hidden ability. I like to understand, listen to others. I like to be of service, intellectual work, psychology, psychiatry, and to learn more to be able to help others because of brotherly love. (Lola, twenty-nine, transgender sex worker)

The deeply emotional connection many transgendered workers had to sex work could be related to the greater overlap between their work, identity, and personal lives. However, transgender workers were more likely than either males or females to express suicidal thoughts, experiencing a drop in energy and a loss of interest in things that once gave them pleasure as a result of the pressure of their transgender status. Many female workers had access to a kind of social support and acceptance in their personal lives that transgender workers did not.

Gender, Alcohol, Drugs and Needles

Some sex workers brought their addictions into the trade and began work in order to support their habit:

I started to work [sexually] for the need of drugs because I used drugs before. I started so I could feed my habit, have a small room and eat, at times not even eat. (Rosamar, forty-five, female sex worker)

The most prevalent occupational risks faced by male sex workers were drug addiction and violence. Many noted a growing connection between drug and alcohol use and their work activities. Thus, I frame addiction as an occupational risk, largely because workers used drugs and alcohol to cope with elevated stress, depression, and violence associated with work. As part of a vicious cycle, addiction is not only a potential outcome of occupational risks, but also increasingly elevates risk in that sex workers then engage in additional sex work in order to feed the addiction. They experience less control over the sexual transaction, which potentially increases risk for violence and STIs, and they deal with even greater shame and guilt because of their addiction.

As is suggested by table 6.12, alcohol and drug use and the use of sex in exchange for either alcohol or drugs were more prominent among males. Male workers were more likely to drink to get drunk at an earlier age, to be drinking to get drunk regularly at the time of this study, and to have sex while under the influence of alcohol. They also began using drugs an average of four years earlier than female and transgender workers. They were more likely than either group to use a variety of street drugs and were more likely than

Table 6.12. Alcohol and Illicit Drug Use (by Gender) (percentages)

	Female	Male	Trans
Age they first got drunk (mean)	17 years	14 years	15 years
Frequently drink to get drunk	53	57	50
Think they have a drinking problem	6	7	19
Frequently have sex while drunk	36	55	50
Have sex to get alcohol	3	26	13
Age they first used illicit drugs (mean)	20 years	16 years	20 years
Frequently use drugs to get high	32	62	63
Think they have a drug problem	14	21	25
Frequently have sex while on drugs	29	55	63
Have sex to get drugs	9	36	31
Types of drugs used:			
Methamphetamine	21	50	44
Marijuana	14	40	31
Cocaine	20	31	25
Heroin	10	10	6
Inhalants	<1	13	6
Ecstasy	0	10	6
Crack cocaine	2	6	13

females or transgenders to use marijuana, crystal methamphetamine, cocaine, inhalants, and ecstasy. Males were just as likely as females to use heroin but were three times more likely to use crack. One out of every two male workers used crystal methamphetamine, widely considered the most popular of the so-called hard drugs available in Tijuana. More than half of them had sex while on drugs, and more than two-thirds were using drugs at the time of this study. As indicated in table 6.13, needle use patterns could also be a particular point of concern, especially among transgender workers. Although needle use in Tijuana was common among all three groups, primarily as a result of the popularity of injectable vitamins, it was highest among transgender workers, who used needles to inject hormones, vitamins, and drugs. In this study, male and transgender workers who shared needles used water, instead of bleach, to clean needles. The purchase of new needles, available at any local pharmacy in Mexico, was the most common practice. The number of needle-injecting drug users in this study was too small to explore more definitively. However, while addiction to intravenous drugs was not a significant factor in the lives of the sex workers participating in this study, it was a greater risk among male and transgender workers than among females. Stereotypes of prostitutes being primarily drug-addicted females just do not apply.

Conclusion

Epidemiological measurements have shown that there is a strong correlation between work venue and risk for STIs (Plumridge et al. 2001; Uribe-Salas et al. 1996), but the importance of class, gender, and sexual orientation in shaping *where* one works is left out of such accounts. As suggested by my findings, social variables are tightly integrated with one another in the sexual and moral geography of the sex industry. As such, work site appears to serve as a proxy for social stratification, making it difficult to control for any one particular variable through statistical (regression) analysis. Further, Mexican epidemiological research on sex work has tended to focus exclusively on sexual risk among female commercial sex workers.[9] Female workers are identified as a potential risk group to be governed by civic authorities[10] but are relatively safer at work because of the harm reduction approach employed by the city, which includes legalization, mandatory screenings, and police protection. However, the coexistence of transgender and male sex workers and the specific nature of gendered risks, sexual or otherwise, are ignored. Such accounts cannot explain how, why, and under what circumstances gender shapes risk for HIV, nor do they account for risk that is not directly related to work practices.

While an increasing body of research examines sexual risk management among female sex workers, the significance of these dynamics to male or transgender sex workers is not well understood. This research does demonstrate that condom use among sex workers is shaped by their categorization of sexual interactions as either noncommercial or commercial[11] and as either regular or casual.[12] The significance of intimacy and trust is not limited to

Table 6.13. Needle Use (by Gender) (percentages)

	Female	Male	Trans
Use needles to inject vitamins, hormones, or illicit drugs	42	4	50
. . . Needle users who share needles	10	20	20
. . . Needle sharers who don't use bleach	50	100	100

noncommercial relationships; the familiarity and comfort that build over time with long-term customers may lay the groundwork for such expectations within commercial relationships. Likewise, early on in a noncommercial relationship, perhaps when the relationship is seen to be more casual, there may not be much of an expectation for fidelity between partners.

Although the intent of much of this research is to shed light on condom use patterns and reasons for not using condoms, such research also helps us understand the role of commercial sexual exchange in the context of longer-term partnerships and sexual networking. My book demonstrates that these relationships are just as meaningful, if not more so, among male and transgender workers in Tijuana.

Some excellent historical and contemporary accounts of the gendered nature of occupational risk for sex workers in other settings are available. Most accounts focus on female sex workers, but some treat male and transgender sex workers as well.[13] The idea of a gendered nature of risk, as discussed in these settings, is applicable to other social and cultural settings. Social context and gender relations do differ, providing specific dynamics within these settings that potentially shape risk behaviors. Unfortunately, few studies take a balanced, comparative approach to gendered risk among all three groups in a particular area.[14] This book contributes to our understanding of these issues by providing such an approach.

Gender diversity structures occupational risk because sex workers are able to exercise varying degrees of personal control in transactions with clients in their decision to work in particular settings and ability to refuse particular customers; they also exercise varying degrees of control in setting the terms of the sexual transaction, including the sexual acts to be performed, the use of condoms, price setting, and time limit.

While the formal sector is highly stratified by class differences between street and club workers, it is made up of primarily heterosexual females who serve male customers. The greater social diversity of the business as a whole, which includes a large informal sector of illegal workers characterized by gender diversity, has not been successfully addressed by municipal authorities or city health policy.

Female, male, and transgender sex workers differ extensively in terms of their demographic backgrounds, structural vulnerability, and social networks and migration activities as well as in their overall approach to work, work experiences, and occupational risks. I have identified the gendered nature of sex work activities further by examining differences in customer solicitation and transaction sites, sexual practices with customers, social relations with customers outside of the work venue, social status and stigma, and risk for work-related depression, violence, drug addiction, and HIV infection.

Whereas female workers face higher rates of work-related stress and depressive symptoms and social stigma related to their work as prostitutes, male and transgender workers face higher rates of work-related sexual risk, customer and police violence, and drug addiction as well as social stigma related to their sexual activities with other males.

There appear to be differing levels of sexual agency between female, male, and transgender workers as a result of their employment in particular sectors. Standardization of sexual exchange, access to professional status and legal venues, and sexual agency appear to be interconnected. Male and transgender sex workers are excluded from the formal system because they do not fall into the more conventional heterosexual female service role which is widely heteronormative, feminized, and homophobic. There is no public acknowledgment that male sex workers, who usually have gay male customers, exist. As a doctor in the city clinic explained, there is no way the city is going to acknowledge or legitimate homosexual behavior among its residents. While there are some transgender workers who register for municipal health services, many work outside of the formal system at greatly increased risk to their physical and mental health. Currently no male sex workers are legal with the city, and their gender-specific and occupational health needs remain unaddressed.

The few ongoing research studies on the sex industry rely on convenience samples of female legal sex workers attending monthly clinic screenings. This formal sector is made up of nearly all female, no male, and a few transgender sex workers, most of whom work in nightclubs, bars, and a few select streets and massage parlors closest to the tourist footpaths near the border. The informal sector, on the other hand, includes male, transgender, and some female sex workers, many of whom work in more clandestine settings, such as gay bars, parks, beaches, smaller massage parlors, and street strolls catering less to tourists than to locals and migrant workers.

Sexual transactions with customers are highly standardized within the formal setting in which most females work. Standardization is quite literally enforced through social sanctions and occasional physical harassment between workers. Although those who charge less than market value or provide sex without condoms or other forms of high-risk sex are able to undercut their competitors, such social sanctions act to discourage behaviors outside the agreed-upon social norms.

The lack of standardized sexual exchanges among male and transgender sex workers, while allowing for a flexibility that was sometimes beneficial to individual sex workers, put many at greater risk in that they had to continually renegotiate their sexual boundaries with customers. Compromises included allowing customers to not use condoms, allowing riskier sex, such as anal sex rather than masturbation or oral sex, and allowing customers to take them to unfamiliar or potentially dangerous areas for the sexual transaction.

With respect to the customer transaction, legal workers have access to a professional status that increases both their sense of agency as well as actual control over the transaction. Whereas the conventional Latin American female role largely encourages sexual passivity and naiveté, sex workers are able to manipulate this role in order to maximize their earnings and reduce occupational risk. In this context, sexual sophistication can be used as a marketing tool rather than a stigmatized attribute. Cleanliness and personal hygiene, aesthetics, regular health screenings, and standardized work practices help workers establish and maintain their professionalized identities. By manipulating this professionalized role and by working in establishments where condom use is promoted and violence and drug use are largely discouraged, female workers are able to minimize the occupational risk to an extent that male and transgender workers are not.

The nature of sex work and occupational risk is clearly gendered. In Tijuana, city policy addresses some of the gender-specific needs of its female workers while leaving its male and transgender workers at greatly increased risk because of their criminal status. Male and transgender workers should be brought into the registration process and allowed to work legally. Officials, of course, are not unaware of the existence of male and female workers. It is doubtful that research assessments of their health needs will change the current policies if the stigma and homophobia which inform them are not addressed. But such assessments are nevertheless a step in the right direction.

Conclusions and Recommendations

The implications of legal status on working conditions and occupational risk are clear. Although previous research on sex work in Mexico suggests a statistical correlation between work venues and risk for STIs,[1] I have demonstrated *how* work venues affect occupational health and safety more generally as well as how legal status shapes who works in which venue. While some comparative research focuses on street versus bar workers, the legality of these venues and the enforcement practices associated with each have been overlooked. In Tijuana, surveillance and policing of those who work illegally has led to increased violence, harassment, and mental health problems. In this setting, illegal status clearly shapes occupational health and safety. My findings support the claims made by sex worker activists: criminalization of sex work *does* negatively impact sex worker health and safety.[2] However, I would go a step further and claim that criminalization does not impact all sex workers equally: it may benefit some while disenfranchising others. One's place within the social world influences how legal status operates in determining occupational risk.

The resources of legal and illegal workers differ, therefore, and the way risks are managed also differs. Legal status and formalization shape a work venue in a way that opens potential avenues in responding to risk, avenues like reliance on and help from hotel staff, coworkers, and police. These avenues, while not completely absent, are less likely to be available to illegal workers in the informal sector. My findings demonstrate that representations of the formal sector tell only half of the story. It is misleading to rely on data from legal sex workers alone. While regulation might be more effective in lessening the severity and prevalence of occupational risks, it exists within a larger context in which sex workers who work outside of this system are criminalized, harassed, policed, and further marginalized while trying to make a living. It is unlikely that the system of regulation will be dismantled anytime soon or that illegal sex work activities will become legal. Although legal status can provide benefits to some workers, it is based on an exclusionary system that increases occupational risks to many while benefiting the few.

This system needs to be more inclusive of those who currently work in the informal sector. Currently, the restrictions against undocumented and under-age workers in the registration process deny protections to those who most need health services. Increased police surveillance leads more to fear, hostility, and evasion on the part of those who most need social services than to greater compliance. It does not encourage registration. Police violence and corruption should not be tolerated, and police should be paid a better wage so that they might be less inclined to extort money from illegal workers. Registration should not be required in order to protect personal civil rights.

While regulation is an effective form of harm reduction in this case, it is also coercive in that specific categories of persons (usually women) are forced to undergo genital health inspections and treatment as well as officially identify themselves as sex workers in order to have the right to work. No other categories of workers are required to undergo these measures, and the need for a mandatory system has yet to be proven. I envision a system in which health card registration is encouraged and rewarded as part of the development of professional identity, something which surely has market value, rather than enforced through the threat of jail, fines, and (unofficially) police violence. Sex workers already employ a variety of strategies to decrease their occupational risk, but policy should focus on improved working conditions that will enable them to make safe choices. In order to decrease the prevalence of STIs, municipal services should encourage regular STI screenings for *all* workers—especially those who, because they don't work within a sex-related industry, are less likely to be aware of their risk for infection.

Public health authorities should reprioritize the areas on which they spend their resources. They should begin to focus on areas that sex workers themselves see as priorities, namely, mental health problems, violence, substance addiction, and unsafe working conditions. STIs, while certainly an occupational risk, are not only easier to manage than other risks sex workers face, but also less prevalent than other health hazards. Because of the authorities' tendency to view prostitutes as vectors of disease rather than as workers facing a variety of occupational hazards, fears about STI have been exaggerated and have led to a regulation policy that doesn't make much sense from the perspective of sex workers themselves. The current pattern of health inspections seems to be shaped more by the politics of tourist-oriented reputation than by the relation between health care and the actual vulnerabilities of workers.

The tendency among most researchers is to treat sex workers as if they had the same legal status (legal, criminal) no matter what their position within a particular legal system. This makes larger, cross-cultural comparisons between those who work within the regulated system and those who work outside of it next to impossible.

Prohibition of sex work, while reducing the visibility of street-based activities, has not eliminated either the supply or demand for commercial sex. Prohibition is difficult to enforce, and it does not address the causal factors that make sex work an attractive option for those with access to limited resources and alternatives. As I have demonstrated, it can also cause harm to individual sex workers, who face increased risk of harassment, extortion, physical and sexual assault, and incarceration. I argue that it also interferes with an individual's right to work and with their ability to care for vulnerable family members. The utilization of the criminal justice system to solve what is essentially a social problem is irresponsible, ineffective, and unethical. Researchers, reformers, and officials need to be more proactive in terms of law, policy, and practice.

As the Tijuana model illustrates, legalization through regulation is one alternative. I would argue that even when it works well, it is far from ideal. First, on a practical level, regulation through mandatory health screenings for STIs addresses neither the broad range of the occupational health needs of sex workers not the health needs of the most vulnerable, those who work outside the system without the protection of the law. Because it screens only a small fraction of sex workers, it is not an adequate mode of disease surveillance. It perpetuates the idea that sex work is a relatively low-risk activity that can be adequately addressed through screening a relatively privileged subgroup of the population for STIs and does not encourage municipal authorities and residents to take any further action. On another level, regulation reinforces existing social inequalities between workers by providing legal and social legitimacy to some workers and not to others. It also reinforces the view that the sex worker's body is an object of public surveillance and control without holding customers, employers, taxi cab drivers, wait staff, bouncers, and others who are involved in and benefit from the sex industry accountable for their own sexual activities and potential to spread infection. The focus on STI and genitalia further reinforces a fragmentary view of women's bodies that parallels the customer's gaze. Last, the clinic is far from a gender-neutral space, making it difficult to imagine a situation in which male, transgender, and female sex workers could feel comfortable receiving services.

What are the alternatives to legalization through regulation? Decriminalization alone, a sort of hands-off approach, is not proactive enough. Sex workers' health could be greatly improved, first, by educating customers, regular male partners, employers, and police and holding them accountable for their role in shaping women's health. In areas in which sex work activities thrive, aggressive community-based health programs can provide integrated, comprehensive health services for all residents. While an emphasis on sexual and reproductive health is warranted, a narrow focus on the sex worker's body is not. Transactional sex exists on a continuum, engaging people from all walks of life at different points of the life cycle, and represents a strategic response to changing life circumstances. Moreover, transactional sex is not always formal or commercial in nature, and many of those who engage in such activities do not consider themselves to be sex workers. For this reason, more dignified and effective reproductive public health services for the general population are in order. In addition, while mental health, substance abuse, and violence are health needs that require attention in their own right, integrated and comprehensive services could better acknowledge the linkages between these health problems and sexual and reproductive health. This approach would be responsible, ethical, effective, and efficient; it would result in disease surveillance that is more responsive to emerging health needs, would promote a more healthful environment in the name of the public good, would promote health behavior among all participants of the industry regardless of their role, and would not infringe on the right to medical privacy. Such services could be met through a combination of sliding scale patient fees and earmarked money from city, state, and private sources. Such preventative services, while costly at first, over time will save in treatment and care costs. They are also the right thing to do. Last, a focus on community health would provide a venue for support groups, community organizing, legal assistance, and assistance for those seeking alternative means of support. Ultimately, sex workers would be best served by an expansion of economic alternatives through job training, literacy programs and education, and microfinance programs.

However, given that sex workers currently must undergo mandatory STI screenings in order to work legally, *accommodation to this model is crucial to sex workers' health and safety.* Those sex workers who refuse or are otherwise unable to accommodate this model clearly face additional health risks as a result of their illegal status. For it is by working legally that sex workers can better avoid risk and hold perpetrators accountable for violence and exploitation. Thus legal status, however it is achieved and agreed upon, offers a framework for how sex workers can expect to be treated. If it is true that social determinants shape working conditions to such an extent, a more clinical framework is not necessarily a useful starting point in generating appropriate public health policy.

Sex Work Activists Debate the Law

Sex work remains a controversial issue, despite its dubious reputation as the world's oldest profession. Even feminists, stalwart defenders of women's rights, are divided. Some feminists argue that legalization of sex work serves to normalize and institutionalize the sexual exploitation of women. Other feminists, including sex worker activists, assert the view that criminalization itself is a form of oppression, one that serves to further stigmatize women, making it more difficult and dangerous for them to make a living as sex workers. Each side of the debate makes assumptions about female agency in relation to their involvement in commercial sexual exchange. Sex workers are themselves deeply divided on this issue. I confess that I find both sides of the debate compelling but also agree with Pheterson (1996), who states the following:

> Firstly, victimization and agency are not mutually exclusive: Women may at times be victimized in their quest for greater agency and at other times be compelled to take transgressive initiative in their attempt to escape constraints. Secondly, such debates are erroneously staged as a numbers game, as if scientific demonstration of a high percentage of violated women or of "free women" would change the critical fact that *both* coerced and autonomous prostitutes are punished by law and stigmatized by society. . . . The menace of male violence is a discriminatory mechanism of social control against women in general . . . [and] controlling women's behavior as a response to male violence is unjustifiable and untenable.

There is growing empirical evidence to support the perspective outlined above. Since the 1980s, feminist ethnographers, particularly those involved in research on gender and sexuality in the context of globalization, have shied away from portrayals of simple hierarchy and dichotomies (male/female, North/South, agent/victim, and so forth) in favor of including a diversity of shifting social locations and flows of power that shape the politics of everyday life (Abu-Lughod 1990, 1993; Kempadoo 1999, 2001; Kempadoo and Doezema 1998). Constable (2003), for example, has written a compelling account of the way in which Filipina and Chinese women involved in correspondence relationships—known in the popular imagination as mail-order brides—make "informed, logical choices from an array of available yet structurally limited options" in negotiating and expressing their agency vis-à-vis their U.S. male correspondents. These ethnographies have been crucial in our understanding of how individuals navigate and negotiate a social world that both facilitates and constrains their actions.

Having spent over two years studying the sex industry firsthand (and many more thinking, reading, and writing about the subject), I remain convinced that the oppression and discrimination faced by women must be fought by expanding, rather than limiting, women's opportunities for social and economic mobility. I cannot in good conscience support a position that limits the freedom of some women, particularly poor, uneducated women with few viable opportunities, in order to "protect" them from objectification and exploitation. And I find a view that treats adult sex worker women as "victims" who require the state to intervene on their behalf, presumably because they cannot act on their own behalf, to be patronizing and outdated. Further, it is my sense that the victimization perspective damages the public's perception of women as liberated, capable adults. It does not promote women's solidarity or recognize that women have differential access to social and economic resources. It does not promote a vision or strategy for social change that women in developing countries or in inner-city America can embrace. As a scientist and a public health activist, I see strong empirical evidence that criminalization increases women's occupational health risks and is antithetical to promoting protective health behaviors.

Criminalization has not eradicated sex work, but it has made it more difficult for sex workers to access appropriate services. A knee-jerk crackdown on sex work drives sex work further underground, rendering street-based sex work less visible or moving it into someone else's jurisdiction. A proactive approach would recognize that more general reforms of social, economic, and health services are required. Substance abuse treatment, mental health care services, job training and educational programs, a safe living and workplace environment, and child care services are desperately needed. Only when these basic needs are met for all women is it fair to expect them to resist sex work as a viable alternative for making ends meet (ironically, given the level of economic instability faced by some women, it's a wonder that sex work *isn't* utilized more often). Those who choose sex work in spite of viable alternatives should also be supported. It is their choice and their right.

The international sex trade, of which Tijuana is a part, poses similar issues. Border crossing for the purposes of sex work is clearly illegal in most countries. In fact, in an effort to prevent this trade, many countries, including the United States, do not permit anyone with a history of sex work to enter the country legally. Although the international sex trade is usually portrayed as the sexual enslaving and criminal trafficking of women and children who are forced to travel against their will and sold into slavery by their parents, it is estimated that, even in Thailand (which is well known for the enslavement of young girls), only 5 percent of the trade can be characterized in this manner (Bales 2002).

The vast majority of international sex work is more rightly characterized as a form of migrant work, sharing a number of commonalities with other forms of illegal migrant labor (Sassen 2002). That is, because of their high degree of mobility and their illegal status, migrant workers are unlikely to have strong support networks to rely upon while working in their host country. They often do not speak the language of the host country, they may be particularly dependent upon their employers (in this case, their pimps), who are likely to exploit them, and they are unlikely to report assault or exploitation to the authorities out of fear that they will be incarcerated or deported because of their illegal status. Again, although migrant workers may choose to engage in sex work as a stepping-stone to international migration (Brennan 2002), travel across international borders to engage in the commercial sex trade (Kempadoo 1998, 1999), or decide to become active in the sex trade after arrival (Sassen 2002), they remain structurally vulnerable and face a narrow degree of autonomy while in their host country. Like sex workers who work domestically, it is the structured nature of their working conditions that poses the greatest risk in terms of occupational health and safety. And, like those who work in their country of origin, it is likely that their legal status is the predominant risk factor in determining their exposure to and ability to address the hazards posed by their work.

Certainly, kidnapping, rape, threats, coercion, and psychological and emotional battering by perpetrators should continue to be illegal and subject to prosecution. These crimes are illegal, whether related to the sex trade or not, and need to be enforced. However, I have yet to see convincing evidence that the criminalization and prosecution of sex workers themselves are effective deterrents to their exploiters. Crackdowns, which generally target only the most visible and vulnerable workers, tend, as noted, to drive sex work further underground. If anything, the treatment of sex workers as criminals increases their vulnerability and makes them easier to exploit.

Regardless of how you stood on these issues prior to reading this book, once you have finished reading it, finished comparing the empirical data contrasting the experiences of prostitutes working legally and those who work illegally and listened to their experiences, you should find yourself rethinking your stance in light of these findings. If you have previously supported a crackdown on sex work in the name of protecting sex workers and their health, you might consider the impact this crackdown had on their lives and life chances. Alternately, if you already support regulation, I urge you to think about how existing regulations could be improved. Regulation is problematic in theory as well as in practice; it has clearly had an impact on sex workers' health and safety. Decriminalization need not include the policing of sexual bodies in the name of public health; regulations designed to protect the public's safety may do so at the expense of sex workers' health and safety. Sex workers, too, are an important part of that public body. They also deserve police protection and public support of their civil and human rights. If regulation further marginalizes those who are the most desperate, then it should not be supported. If regulation focuses only on the sexual aspects of work and neglects the psychological, emotional, and safety concerns of sex workers, then it should not be supported. Workplace regulations should, first and foremost, protect workers and empower them to protect themselves. The existing framework in Tijuana has too many problems to be considered an adequate solution.

The Tijuana Regulatory Model

As I have tried to demonstrate, the use of a female-oriented, for-profit clinic to provide legal registration in the form of mandatory health screenings, registration, and health cards is problematic. Although the provision of health care and treatment for sex workers is important and necessary, the Tijuana model of legalization is dangerous for a number of reasons.

First, strict registration requirements and inconsistent health inspections largely exclude or discourage those sex workers who are the most vulnerable. As the only mechanism for obtaining legal work, this regime forces those who are the most vulnerable to continue to work illegally and continue to be subjected to greater occupational risks than those who work legally. Further, this approach renders the lives of illegal workers invisible, making it impossible to identify trends in health outcomes and to provide targeted services to those in need. Outside of street outreach provided by local AIDS activists, there is no mechanism in place to address the health needs of those who work illegally.

Second, the focus on screening and treating of STIs neglects important aspects of sex workers' occupational health, health problems that are both more prevalent than STIs and that are perceived as more significant by sex workers—among these are violence, clinical depression, and addiction.

Third, although the standard of care has risen over the past decade, some examinations are still done by visual inspection, and screening and treatment for some of the most prevalent STIs, such as chlamydia, are not provided. A general antibiotic is given for all signs of infection; no laboratory diagnosis is made. Sex workers have lobbied hard for improved services, including the elimination of group gynecological exams and the provision of Pap smears for the detection of cervical cancer. However, there is no regulatory body to ensure that the city sex worker clinic meets the current standard of care offered other citizens.

Fourth, sex workers complain that services at the city clinic are more expensive and less reliable than those at private health services. Because they are not allowed to select their own medical provider, many visit private doctors in conjunction with city services, resulting in duplication of services and greater economic burden.

Fifth, many sex workers find their monthly visits to the city clinic, which provides services exclusively to sex workers, embarrassing, as their medical privacy is compromised. Registration makes their medical records subject to scrutiny by employers, police, and the courts — many sex workers would rather go to jail or pay a fine than be subjected to this scrutiny. Because the clinic is located in a quiet residential neighborhood with no other commercial services, merely being dropped off in front of the facility by a taxi driver can be an uncomfortable experience. In addition, all services are provided under the workers' legal names, and their names are called out in the waiting room when the doctor is ready to see them and when the prescription area has prepared their antibiotic. As employers, police, inspectors, and fellow sex workers can all become aware of a sex worker's infection status, sex workers not unreasonably fear their neighbors and family members will also find out. Although the city clinic is not connected to a shared computer network, many sex workers believe that their name goes into a central computer database that will reveal their registration status to any policeman, medical provider, potential employer, or immigration official. Unless this approach changes, sex workers will continue to protect their social status by not registering and accessing services.

Regulatory services by the city clinic have multiple areas of opportunity. First, the clinic should be person centered rather than disease centered. A holistic community health center would be more effective than a center focused solely on genital infections. By addressing competing risks, a holistic center would bring about a lowering of the risk of sexual infection. The approach is also more humane and would be held as more legitimate among sex workers, who often resent the intrusion of civic authorities into their private activities. Targeting by clinics through health card registration, while annoying, inconvenient, embarrassing, and certainly politically controversial, does have the very real effect of providing private sexual and reproductive health services (though in reality they are far from perfect) to a small segment of a vast uninsured population that relies on an impoverished public health system.

Were it run more effectively and more creatively, the registration process and clinical space could facilitate the development of a more positive experience for sex workers and more adequately address the needs of sex workers as they see them.

The approach that stresses harm reduction has been successful in a large sector of the industry. However, the city clinic should be more inclusive of diverse subgroups and special needs, which would include allowing and encouraging registration among male and transgender sex workers and youth sex workers, particularly those ages sixteen and over. A clinic specifically serving males, or at least a staff trained to deal with the special needs of male and transgender workers, could encourage their registration and utilization of services. Changes can also be made to make the regulatory system less coercive, while still fulfilling the public relations needs of civic authorities. Outreach workers can do on-site workshops or training to encourage registration. Peer outreach workers, instead of health inspectors, would establish more trust and encourage communication and leadership among peers. Support services in the form of individual and group therapy are essential unmet needs among sex workers. Urinary tests for STIS, including chlamydia, should be used rather than visual inspection. Concern for fertility complications should be as important as potential infection of customers. Finally, teaching of needle safety for the injection of hormones and vitamins as well as drugs continues to be important among this population.

Every attempt should be made to encourage registration and regular health checkups. Incentives, not punishment, would encourage registration without the negative effects of police violence and extortion faced by illegal workers. An inexpensive flyer explaining the legal rights of sex workers could reach a variety of workers. This flyer should include an illustration of how registration helps protect the civil rights of workers. The cost of health services should be illustrated in comparison with the cost of police fines and harassment and the cost of private treatment services. Corruption among police should be censured, and there should be a committee or mediator to handle complaints confidentially. The costs of instituting these changes would be far less than those of an HIV/AIDS epidemic and a drop in tourism.

Sex workers deserve to be treated with dignity, they deserve the same standard of care provided to other kinds of workers, they deserve to be treated as whole human beings with health needs that go beyond their genitalia, they deserve the right to choose their medical providers, and they deserve the same privacy regarding medical matters that is given other citizens. As it stands, the Tijuana model falls short of these expectations.

Notes

Introduction

1. An excellent collection and review of feminist geography can be found in Nelson and Seager (2004).

2. The International Labor Organization estimates that up to 1.5 percent of the world's female population is engaged in commercial sex work (Lim 1998).

3. A recent news article argues that the brothel industry is one of the only recession-proof industries (CNN Money 2002). Signs of growing profitability and acceptance include the integration of the pornography industry with cable and hotel conglomerates in the United States, and the world's first publicly listed brothel to sell shares to stockholders.

4. See, for example, Anglin (1998); Baer et al. (1986); Baer et al. (2003); Doyal (1995); Escobar (1995); Farmer (1992, 1999, 2004); Farmer et al. (1996); Herdt (1997); Goldstein (1994); Parker (1991, 1999); Parker et al. (2000); Singer (1990, 1991, 1994, 1998, 2001); and Sobo (1995).

5. These interviews took place with health care providers, advocates, epidemiologists, psychologists, economists, historians, and the secretary of tourism for Baja California. They helped me understand and clarify a variety of aspects of the sex industry that would have been impossible otherwise. For many of these interviews, a return visit was needed to collect additional information or clarify information provided previously. This process, while it revealed shared or disputed understandings of the sex industry in Tijuana, was extremely time intensive because of scheduling and transportation issues. All collaborators received a copy of my research findings in compensation for their time and efforts.

6. I made some exclusions on the basis of practicality or access. To remain more focused, these targeted samples do not include outlying areas of the city, where sex workers sometimes go to work (i.e., smaller red light neighborhoods in other areas of Tijuana-La Mesa, La Presa, etc.; or the nearby towns of Tecate, Rosarito, and Ensenada). I also assessed work venues and locations as potential recruitment sites in terms of ease of access and personal danger. There were some areas, such as the fence, wash, gutters, tunnels, and underpasses, which I decided were too dangerous.

Last, I did not include less formal sex workers (part-time occasional work, sex with casual partners for money or presents) or retired sex workers. Only full-time sex workers who relied primarily on their income from sex work during the previous six months were recruited for this study. Other workers were excluded as a result of various events in the field. I failed to recruit participants using ads for call services (newspaper, Internet, escort agencies). Workers in this area are notoriously difficult to reach, as they have built-in strategies meant to ensure confidentiality. I approached eighteen call service workers by phone, and all declined a request for an interview. I did not approach sex workers working on the beach in my neighborhood because they were involved in a number of relationships within my neighborhood social network. They were generally reluctant to identify themselves as sex workers in their social circle (outside of work), and I felt their confidentiality would potentially be compromised by participation in this study.

7. See Jensen and Rodgers (2001) and Yin (1994) on the general importance and use of the case study method.

8. After an initial training on specimen collection, saliva samples were collected using Orasure and then transported to the San Diego County Health Department for testing on a weekly basis. The HIV-1 antibody status of saliva samples was tested using enzyme-linked immunosorbent assay and confirmed by Western blot. Participant results were linked to surveys through a unique numerical code, given to each participant so that they could retrieve their test result. All participants returned for their test results and received follow-up counseling.

9. Illegal sex workers were less likely to have ever received an HIV test and less likely to have access to municipal or private health services. HIV testing was viewed as a valuable, tangible contribution by participants; even legal workers who had recently received HIV tests from the city clinic specifically requested HIV tests through this study as a sort of second opinion. There is widespread (not completely unfounded) mistrust of the quality of city health services.

10. NUD*IST (Non-numerical Unstructured Data Indexing, Searching, and Theorizing) is used to generate new theories or revise existing theories. It is used to browse and code categories and subcategories within narratives, to index hierarchically, to identify words and patterns to create an index, and to add memos to codes and categories. See Richards and Richards (1991).

Chapter One

1. The best online resource for pictures from this era can be found at http://www.digthatcrazyfarout.com/oldtj/. This slide-show collection presents postcards, photos, and advertisements from the era. The San Diego Historical Society has in its collection vintage postcards illustrating how Tijuana was marketed to tourists during the Prohibition era. Finally, the *Journal of San Diego History* has published a number of well-documented pieces complete with photographs and postcards, which can be viewed online (see http://www.sandiegohistory.org/journal/2002-3/frontierimages .htm).

Chapter Two

1. HIV/AIDS care and treatment are limited. Due to budget constraints, hospice care is provided by volunteers, and some small organizations rely on donated antiretrovirals from the United States. Limited public funds are able to provide drug treatment for a small portion of women with young children.

2. Lustig (1992) provides comprehensive coverage of the economic crisis during the 1970s and 1980s that placed Mexico in a position of dependency on foreign loans and trade. According to Lustig, agreements with the World Bank and the International Monetary Fund required structural adjustments including privatization; price, wage, and exchange rate controls; the relaxation of environmental and labor force regulations; and the acceleration of trade liberalization through the maintenance of high "real" interest rates and the reduction of foreign investment regulations. These adjustments succeeded in attracting foreign investors looking to enhance their comparative advantage in the global market. The Mexican government hoped this agreement would help stabilize a devastated economy by protecting against high rates of inflation and maintaining the peso.

3. The North American Free Trade Agreement (NAFTA) and other neoliberal trade policies have drawn an estimated nine million people to the border region to work in the thousands of manufacturing and assembly plants now established there (La Botz 1994). The global assembly line demands a fragmented, global production process wherein product design, production, assembly, and distribution occur in separate locations in order to increase profits (Peña 1997). A variety of factors influenced foreign investors in their choice of Mexico as a site for industrialization: extremely low real wages; lax occupational and environmental regulations (those regulations that are in place are rarely enforced); a highly flexible workplace (either no unions or compliant unions which play little role on the shop floor); a large, continually replenished labor pool with little work experience; and a host of tax and tariff advantages provided by the Mexican government to attract foreign capital.

4. See Nevins (2002) for an excellent review of border policing trends. Also see Davidson (2000) and Urea (1993) for a more literary approach to these issues.

Chapter Three

1. A subjective measurement of the changing quality of life is summed up by Barlett and Brown (1985: 25): "In rural areas throughout the world, increased agricultural production spurred on by the expansion of a world market has significantly changed people's lives. For most farmers, this progress has been possible only with some real costs—trade-offs—in traditional values and life satisfaction. From an anthropological view, economic development can bring increases in perceived needs that can never be satisfied. As cultures change through increased agricultural production, people may have more material possessions but be less satisfied."

2. This may be due to a reduced need for additional management and protection of street workers within this type of institutionalized setting.

3. Some sex workers discuss the inverse relationship between not being picked

and the blow to their self-esteem. Investments in body modifications, dieting, etc., which help make sex workers more competitive on the market, are often directly related to these phenomena.

4. Similar comparisons could be made to U.S. cities like Las Vegas and Reno, Nevada.

5. My discussion here is influenced by the work of Safa (1995), who examines the contradictions involved in female paid employment and conventional gender roles among female Caribbean industrial workers.

6. See O'Dougherty (2002) on the social status of home ownership in Latin America.

7. See Bourgois (1995) for a similar argument about the class aspirations of drug dealers in Spanish Harlem.

8. Similar accounts have been given by sex workers in the United States, which is dominated by a consumer-oriented culture. Because Mexico is a poor country, this perspective is usually ignored by research.

9. See especially Chapkis (1997), Delacoste and Alexander (1998), Kempadoo and Doezema (1998), and Nagle (1997).

10. See Burana (2001), Eaves (2002), Langley (1997), and Sycamore (2000), for just a few examples.

Chapter Four

1. In Nevada, the formal sector of legal sex work takes place in rural brothels in particular counties, often a long drive from any town or city, whereas the informal sector (which is illegal) occurs in more densely populated areas via street work and escort services.

Chapter Five

1. In Mexico and especially among Latinos in Tijuana and Los Angeles, snake oil is a popular folk remedy for AIDS, cancer, diabetes, and arthritis. It is available through herbal vendors like these as well as in pharmacies and is occasionally responsible for salmonella infection. See Waterman et al. (1990).

2. Although the clinic's policy was to give all new registrants an HIV knowledge, attitude, and practices test, the medical records for the year 2000, which I consulted, revealed that only half had completed these tests. The test is provided by a social worker who was available only on certain days of the week. If a registrant came to be tested on a day when the social worker was not in, he or she would not receive the test.

3. This points to the importance of measuring the frequency and severity of violence, rather than simply asking if someone has ever experienced it.

4. While these incidents were interpreted as robbery by my participants, I would define this as both rape and robbery because the sex worker has not consented to have sex except under a particular condition (being paid). If payment is withheld or taken back, then the sex is nonconsensual.

5. There was no official record made of any of these incidents, and I did not try to confirm them for fear that the people who told me might suffer retaliation. I do believe that business owners might engage in cover-ups out of fear of bad publicity (and potential litigation) for providing an unsafe environment. Also, they would not want to alarm other workers, who might leave town or go to work for a competitor.

6. I believe this is due to the nature of their work sites and to the requirements of management—bars and nightclubs require workers to drink with customers, and some require even that the worker meet a quota, that is, the customer must buy a certain number of drinks before they go to the room.

7. For example, see Ahmed et al. (2003), Chen et al. (2000), Erbelding (2003), and Mbizvo et al. (2002).

8. For examples, see Morisky et al. (1998).

9. Silicone-based lubricants are hard to find in Tijuana, and most workers aren't aware that they exist. Therefore, I have left discussion of these lubricants out of my analysis.

10. A miniworkshop on lubricants, along with a set of flavored and scented water-based lubricants, was provided to each participant after he or she was interviewed. Pamphlets about condom use and lubricants (in Spanish) were also provided.

11. For examples, see Farmer et al. (1996), Goldstein (1994), Herdt (1997), Icko-vicks and Rodin (1992), and Sacks (1996).

12. See Bandura (1994) and Fisher et al. (1999).

13. See Patton (1996) for an excellent history of HIV/AIDS policies and approaches in the United States.

14. See Castañeda et al. (1996), Dorfman et al. (1992), and Moore et al. (1995).

15. See Decarlo et al. (1996), Campbell (1991), Cohen and Coyle (1990), Lamptey (1991), and Leonard and Thistlewaite (1990).

16. See Decarlo et al. (1996), Farmer et al. (1996), and Ickovicks and Rodin (1992).

17. A doctor at the STI clinic told me that approximately four legal workers per year become infected with HIV.

18. The anthropological fascination with despatialized, transnational, diasporic, virtual, and imagined communities belied the significance of space and the accompanying spatial politics in constraining or building community relations. While this turn in anthropology has shown us that community spaces need not be tied to a physical geography in all cases, spatial politics and the social use of physical space need to be foregrounded analytically, as has been done by Setha Low and others (1999; 2000).

Chapter Six

1. In this study, I use the word *transgender* to refer to male-to-female trans-genders, males who dress, live, or work as females—and who may modify their bodies in order to acquire female sex characteristics and service heterosexually defined male desire. There were no female-to-male transgenders (females who dress, live, or work as males) in this study, and I did not meet any during my fieldwork.

2. See Barr et al. 1996; ECPAT (1996); IBCR (1998a, 1998b); and Longford (1995).

3. The experience sex workers had of returning home after working in Tijuana and the effect that their work and income had on family structure (gendered power relations, for example) were found to be so complex and interesting as to require a separate research study. Ideally, this study would include following sex workers to their sending communities, observing the tension between their stigmatized social status and their economic contributions, interviewing family and community members, and identifying the role of gender norms and expectations in the reintegration process (a set of techniques which would fall squarely into multisite ethnography). My hypothesis for such a study is that in the case of female sex workers at least there is bound to be extreme tension between her and her male kin, especially her father or husband, as her status of becoming the family breadwinner becomes apparent. Understanding the negotiation of gender roles in these circumstances would bring something completely new to the field and would require long-term commitment to developing field relationships that could support such intense observation and interviewing. Again, while fascinating and relevant to understanding the experiences of sex workers, I had neither the time nor resources to explore this phenomenon as it emerged from my conversations with sex workers.

4. Functional bisexuality is generally understood as a dynamic specific to gender relations in Latin America, especially the dynamics involved in masculinity (machismo) and the world of men. In its most common understanding, such a dynamic differentiates between the active/passive sexual partner (the anal inserter is considered active, and the receiver is considered passive). This dynamic includes gender performance—whereas an effeminate male is perceived as passive and therefore gay, a male who acts macho (aggressive, virile, etc.) is considered active and not necessarily gay. See Parker (1991) and Prieur (1998) for more detailed discussions. Parker's later work (1999) demonstrates that in Latin America this gender dynamic can also be applied toward understanding male sex work.

5. Some of the best explanations of these factors among women include Doyal (1995), Farmer et al. (1996), Ickovicks and Rodin (1992), and Sobo (1995).

6. Condom use can be a choice between a "biological death" from AIDS and a "social death" in which childbearing is tightly linked to social status, respect, and economic stability.

7. See, for example, Sobo's (1995) work on monogamy narratives among inner-city women.

8. See Stevens (1973) for an introduction to marianismo.

9. See Calderon-Jaimes et al. (1994); Conde-Gonzalez et al. (1999); Hernandez-Giron et al. (1998); Juárez-Figueroa et al. (1998); Juárez-Figueroa et al. (2001); and Uribe-Salas et al. (1995).

10. The premise of targeting female commercial sex workers as vectors for HIV transmission is based on methodologically flawed research and stereotypes which paint women as vectors of disease. In fact, numerous studies have shown that in the absence of drug addiction, female sex workers are no more likely to be infected than other sorts of workers. See Sacks (1996) for a comprehensive review.

11. Other research consistently supports this point. Some examples of these studies include Albert et al. 1998; Campbell (1991); CDC (1987); Cusick (1998); Day and Ward (1990); Green et al. (1993); Highcrest and Maki (1992); Hooykaas et al.

(1989); Jackson et al. (1992); McKeganey and Barnard (1992); McLeod (1982); van den Hoek et al. (1998); Venema and Visser (1990); and Waddell (1996).

12. See, for example, Morris (1995) and Outwater et al. (2000). Also see Leonard and Ross (1997) as one of many examples on the differentiation between regular and casual partners and condom use patterns among non–sex workers.

13. See, for example, Bloor and McKeganey (1990); Boles and Elifson 1994; Browne and Minichiello (1995); de Graaf and Vanwesenbeeck (1994); Mathews (1987); Morse et al. (1992); Odo and Hawelu (2001); West (1993); and Wiessing (1999).

14. Some that do include Weinberg et al. (1999); Harcourt et al. (2001); and Valera et al. (2001).

Conclusion

1. See Carrier et al. (1989); Conde-Gonzalez et al. (1999); Hernandez-Giron et al. (1998); and Uribe-Salas et al. (1995).

2. See, in particular, Chapkis (1997), Delacoste and Alexander (1998), and Pheterson (1996).

Glossary

fichar/fichara   drinking and dancing with customers for tips

gastitos   little expenses

indígena   of indigenous ancestry; also called *indios/as*

Latino/Latina   male or female of Hispanic descent; not representative of a particular nationality

mexicana   female Mexican national

polleros   literally, "chicken rancher"—those who smuggle illegal immigrants into the United States; also called *coyotes*

pollos   literally, "chickens"—those who try to cross into the United States illegally

Zona Norte   literally, "Northern Zone"—the name of the neighborhood located between the border fence, footpath, and Avenida Revolución

zona de tolerancia   literally, "tolerance zone"—the nickname given to zoned commercial districts where sex work is tolerated by police; also called *la zona roja*, or "red-light district"

Bibliography

Abu-Lughod, Lila. 1990. "The Romance of Resistance: Tracing Transformations of Power through Bedouin Women." *American Ethnologist* 17(1): 41–55.

———. 1993. *Writing Women's Worlds: Bedouin Stories*. Berkeley: University of California Press.

Ahmed H. J., J. Mbwana, E. Gunnarsson, K. Ahlman, C. Guerino, L. A. Svensson, F. Mhalu, and T. Lagergard. 2003. "Etiology of Genital Ulcer Disease and Association with Human Immunodeficiency Virus Infection in Two Tanzanian Cities." *Sexually Transmitted Disease* 30(2): 114–119.

Albert, A. E., D. L. Warner, R. A. Hatcher, J. Trussell, and C. Bennett. 1995. "Condom Use among Female Commercial Sex Workers in Nevada's Legal Brothels." *American Journal of Public Health* 85(11): 1514–1520. Review.

Albert, A. E., D. L. Warner, and R. A. Hatcher. 1998. "Facilitating Condom Use with Clients during Commercial Sex in Nevada's Legal Brothels." *American Journal of Public Health* 88(4): 643–647.

Albert, Alexa. 2001. *Brothel: Mustang Ranch and Its Women*. New York: Random House.

Alvarado-Esquivel, C., A. Garcia-Villanueva, D. E. Castruita-Limones, F. J. Cardosa-Nevarez, and R. Ruiz-Astorga. 2000. ["Prevalence of Chlamydia trachomatis infection in legal prostitutes in the city of Durango, Mexico"]. *Salud Pública Mexico* 42(1): 43–47.

Anglin, Mary. 1998. "Feminist Perspectives on Structural Violence." *Identities* 5(2): 145–151.

Baer, Hans, Merrill Singer, and John Johnsen. 1986. "Toward a Critical Medical Anthropology." *Social Science and Medicine* 23(2): 95–98.

Baer, Hans, Merrill Singer, and Ida Susser. 2003. *Medical Anthropology and the World System: A Critical Perspective*. 2d edition. Westport: Praeger.

Baja Exhibit. 2001. Exhibit on the History of Baja California: Centro Cultural. Tijuana, Mexico.

Bales, Kevin. 2002. "Because She Looks Like a Child." In *Global Woman: Nannies, Maids, and Sex Workers in the New Economy*, edited by Barbara Ehrenreich and Arlie Russell Hochschild. New York: Metropolitan Books.

Bandura, A. 1994. "Social Cognitive Theory and Exercise of Control over HIV Infection." In *Preventing AIDS: Theories and Methods of Behavioral Interventions,* edited by R. J. DiClemente. New York: Plenum Press.

Barlett, Peggy, and Peter Brown. 1985. "Agricultural Development and the Quality of Life: An Anthropological View." *Agriculture and Human Values* 2(1): 28–35.

Barr, C. W., M. Clayton, J. Epstein, M. Ingwerson, and J. Matloff. 1996. *Child Sex Trade: Battling a Scourge.* Boston: Christian Science Publishing.

BBC News. 2002. Mexico's Transvestite Ban Draws Gay Protest. http://news.bbc .co.uk/1/hi/world/americas/2402571.stm

Bloor, M., and N. McKeganey. 1990. "An Ethnographic Study of HIV-Related Risk Practices Among Glasgow Rent Boys and Their Clients: Report of a Pilot Study." *AIDS Care* 2(1): 17–24.

Bourgois, Phillipe. 1995. *In Search of Respect: Selling Crack in El Barrio.* New York: Cambridge University Press.

Boles, J., and K. W. Elifson. 1994. "The Social Organization of Transvestite Prostitution and AIDS." *Social Science and Medicine* 39: 85–93.

Bolton, Ralph. 1995. "Tricks, Friends, and Lovers: Erotic Encounters in the Field." In *Taboo: Sex, Identity, and Erotic Subjectivity in Anthropological Fieldwork,* edited by Don Kulick and Margaret Willson, 140–167. London: Routledge.

Brennan, Denise. 2002. "Selling Sex for Visas: Sex Tourism as a Stepping-stone to International Migration." In *Global Woman: Nannies, Maids, and Sex Workers in the New Economy,* edited by Barbara Ehrenreich and Arlie Russell Hochschild. New York: Metropolitan Books.

Browne, J., and V. Minichiello. 1995. "The Social Meanings behind Male Sex Work: Implications for Sexual Interactions." *British Journal of Sociology* 46(4): 598–614.

Calderón-Jaimes, E., C. Conde-González, L. Juárez Figueroa, P. Uribe-Zúñiga, F. Uribe-Salas, M. Olamendi-Portugal, and M. Hernandez-Avila. 1994. ["Prevalence of antitreponemal antibodies in 3,098 female prostitutes in Mexico City"]. *Revista de Investigación Clínica* 46(6): 431–436.

Campbell, C. A. 1991. "Prostitution, AIDS, and Preventive Health Behavior." *Social Science and Medicine* 32(12): 1367–1378.

Carrier, J. M. 1989. "Sexual Behavior and Spread of AIDS in Mexico." *Medical Anthropology* 10(2–3): 129–142.

———. 1999. "Reflections on Ethical Problems Encountered in Field Research on Mexican Male Homosexuality: 1968 to Present." *Culture, Health and Sexuality* 1(3): 207–222.

Castañeda, X., V. Ortiz, B. Allen, C. García, and M. Hernández-Avila. 1996. "Sex Masks: The Double Life of Female Commercial Sex Workers in Mexico City." *Culture, Medicine, and Psychiatry* 20(2): 229–247.

CDC, Centers for Disease Control and Prevention. 1987. "Antibody to Human Immunodeficiency Virus in Female Prostitutes." *Morbidity and Mortality Weekly Report* 36: 157–161.

———. 2001. Chlamydia—CDC Fact Sheet http://www.cdc.gov/std/Chlamydia/ STDFact-Chlamydia.htm

Chapkis, Wendy. 1997. *Live Sex Acts: Women Performing Erotic Labor.* New York: Routledge.

Chen, C. Y., R. C. Ballard, C. M. Beck-Sague, Y. Dangor, F. Radebe, S. Schmid,

J. B. Weiss, V. Tshabalala, G. Fehler, Y. Htun, and S. A. Morse. 2000. "Human Immunodeficiency Virus Infection and Genital Ulcer Disease in South Africa: The Herpetic Connection." *Sexually Transmitted Disease* 27(1): 21–29.

CNN Money. 2002. "Australian Brothel Readies IPO: Bordello Seeks to Raise $5M by Offering 'Recession-Proof' Opportunity." December 13.

Cockcroft, James D. 1986. *Outlaws in the Promised Land: Mexican Immigrant Workers and America's Future.* New York: Grove Press.

Cohen, J. B., and S. L. Coyle. 1990. "Interventions for Female Prostitutes." In *AIDS: The Second Decade*, edited by H. G. Miller. Washington: National Academy Press.

Conde-González, C. J., L. Juárez-Figueroa, F. Uribe-Salas, P. Hernández-Nevarez, D. S. Schmid, E. Calderón, and M. Hernández-Avila. 1999. "Analysis of Herpes Simplex Virus 1 and 2 Infection in Women with High Risk Sexual Behavior in Mexico." *International Journal of Epidemiology* 28(3): 571–576.

Connell, Patricia. 1997. "Understanding Victimization and Agency: Considerations of Race, Class and Gender." *PoLAR: Political and Legal Anthropology Review* 20(2): 115–143.

Constable, Nicole. 2003. *Romance on a Global Stage: Pen Pals, Virtual Ethnography, and Mail Order Marriages.* Berkeley: University of California Press.

Crenshaw, K. W. (1994). "Mapping the Margins: Intersectionality, Identity Politics, and Violence Against Women of Colour." In *The Public Nature of Private Violence*, edited by M. A. Fineman and R. Mykitiuk. New York: Routledge.

Cusick, L. 1998. "Non-use of Condoms by Prostitute Women." *AIDS Care* 10(2): 133–146.

Cwikel, J., B. Chudakov, M. Paikin, K. Agmon, and R. H. Belmaker. 2004. "Trafficked Female Sex Workers Awaiting Deportation: Comparison with Brothel Workers." *Archives of Women's Mental Health* 7(4): 243–250.

Day, Sophie, and Helen Ward. 1990. "The Praed Street Project: A Cohort of Prostitute Women in London." In *AIDS, Drugs, and Prostitution*, edited by M. Plant. London: Tavistock Routledge.

Davidson, Miriam. 2000. *Lives on the Line: Dispatches from the U.S.–Mexico Border.* Tucson: University of Arizona Press.

de Graaf, I. Vanwesenbeeck, G. van Zessen, C. J. Straver, and J. H. Visser. 1993. "The Effectiveness of Condom Use in Heterosexual Prostitution in The Netherlands." *AIDS* 7(2): 265–269.

de Graaf, R., and I. Vanwesenbeeck. 1994. "Male Prostitutes and Safe Sex: Different Settings, Different Risks." *AIDS Care* 6(3): 277–289.

Decarlo, Pamela, Priscilla Alexander, and Henry Hsu. 1996. What Are Sex Workers' HIV Prevention Needs? Center for AIDS Prevention Studies at the University of California San Francisco. http://www.caps.ucsf.edu/pubs/FS/prosttext.php

Delacoste, Frédérique, and Priscilla Alexander. 1998. *Sex Work: Writings by Women in the Sex Industry.* San Francisco: Cleis Press.

Dorfman, L. E., P. A. Derish, and J. B. Cohen. 1992. "Hey Girlfriend: An Evaluation of AIDS Prevention among Women in the Sex Industry." *Health Education Quarterly* 19: 25–40.

Doyal, Lesley. 1995. *What Makes Women Sick: Gender and the Political Economy of Health.* New Brunswick: Rutgers University Press.

Eaves, Elisabeth. 2002. *Bare: On Women, Dancing, Sex, and Power.* Westminster: Knopf.

ECPAT (End Child Prostitution, Child Pornography, and the Trafficking of Children for Sexual Exploitation). 1996. Europe and North America Regional Profile. Stockholm, Sweden: World Congress against Commercial Sexual Exploitation of Children.

Erbelding, E. 2003. "2001 Syphilis Rates Show Increase: Does this Portend a New Wave of HIV Infection?" *Hopkins HIV Report* 15(1): 15.

Escobar, Arturo. 1995. *Encountering Development: The Making and Unmaking of the Third World.* Princeton: Princeton University Press.

Farmer, Paul. 1992. *AIDS and Accusation: Haiti and the Geography of Blame.* Berkeley: University of California Press.

———. 1999. *Infections and Inequalities: The Modern Plagues.* Berkeley: University of California Press.

———. 2004. "Sidney W. Mintz Lecture for 2001: An Anthropology of Structural Violence." *Current Anthropology* 45(3): 305-325.

Farmer, Paul, M. Conners, and Janie Simmons, eds. 1996. *Women, Poverty, and AIDS: Sex, Drugs, and Structural Violence.* Monroe, Me.: Common Courage Press.

Fisher, W. A., S. S. Williams, J. D. Fisher, and T. E. Malloy. 1999. "Understanding AIDS Risk Behavior among Sexually Active Urban Adolescents: An Empirical Test of the Information-Motivation-Behavioral Skills Model." *AIDS and Behavior* 3(1): 13-23.

Frank, Katherine. 2002. *G-Strings and Sympathy: Strip Club Regulars and Male Desire.* Durham: Duke University Press.

Ganster, Paul. 1999. *Tijuana, Basic Information.* Vol. 2003. San Diego State University, Institute for Regional Studies of the Californias. http://www-rohan.sdsu.edu/~irsc/tjreport/tj1.html

Goldstein, Donna M. 1994. "AIDS and Women in Brazil: The Emerging Problem." *Social Science and Medicine* 39(7): 919-929.

Green, S. T., D. J. Goldberg, P. R. Christie, M. Frischer, A. Thomson, S. V. Carr, and A. Taylor. 1993. "Female Streetworker-Prostitutes in Glasgow: A Descriptive Study of Their Lifestyle." *AIDS Care* 5: 321-335.

Harcourt, C., I. van Beek, J. Heslop, M. McMahon, and B. Donovan. 2001. "The Health and Welfare Needs of Female and Transgender Street Sex Workers in New South Wales." *Australian and New Zealand Journal of Public Health* 25(1): 84-89.

Harris, Bruce. 1997. "The Situation of Street Children in Latin America." Latin American Programmes, Casa Alianza/Covenant House Latin America, 9 October.

Health and Medicine Week. 2004. "Health Officials Urge Government to Ratify U.N. Treaty on People." *Health and Medicine Week,* March 15: 491-493.

Herdt, Gilbert, ed. 1997. *Sexual Cultures and Migration in the Era of AIDS: Anthropological and Demographic Perspectives.* Oxford: Oxford University Press.

Hernández-Girón, C. A., A. Cruz-Valdez, L. J. Figueroa, and M. Hernández-Avila. 1998. ["Prevalence and risk factors associated with syphilis in women"]. *Revista de Salud Pública* 32(6): 579-586.

Heyman, J. M., and H. Campbell. 2004. "Recent Research on the U.S.–Mexico Border." *Latin American Research Review* 39(3): 205-220.

Highcrest, A., and K. Maki. 1992. "Prostitutes: AIDS Prevention in Their Private

Lives." VIII International Conference on AIDS/III STD World Congress, Amsterdam, The Netherlands.

Hooykaas, C., J. van der Pligt, G. J. van Doornum, M. M. van der Linden, and R. A. Coutinho. 1989. "Heterosexuals at Risk for HIV: Differences between Private and Commercial Partners in Sexual Behavior and Condom Use." *AIDS* 3(8): 525–532.

Hughes, Donna M., Laura Joy Sporcic, Nadine Z. Mendelsohn, and Vanessa Chirgwin. 1999. "The Factbook on Global Sexual Exploitation." Coalition Against Trafficking in Women. http://www.uri.edu/artsci/wms/hughes/factbook.htm

Ickovics, J., and J. Rodin. 1992. "Women and AIDS in the United States: Epidemiology, Natural History, and Mediating Mechanisms." *Health Psychology* 11(1).

IBCR, International Bureau for Children's Rights. 1998a. "Report of Public Hearings." Fortaleza, Brazil: International Dimensions of Child Sexual Exploitation.

———. 1998b. "Report of Public Hearing." Bangkok, Thailand: International Dimensions of Child Sexual Exploitation.

Ichikawa, S., H. Ohya, M. Kihara, T. M. Sankary, M. Kihara, M. Imai, and M. Kondo. 1999. ["The survey of HIV infection among clients of foreign female prostitutes in Tokyo metropolitan]. [Article in Japanese]. *Nippon Koshu Eisei Zasshi* 46(8): 638–643.

Jackson, L., A. Highcrest, and R. A. Coates. 1992. "Varied Potential Risks of HIV Infection Among Prostitutes." *Social Science and Medicine* 35: 281–286.

Jensen, Jason L., and Robert Rodgers. 2001. "Cumulating the Intellectual Gold of Case Study Research." *Public Administration Review* 61(2): 236–246.

Juárez-Figueroa, L. A., C. M. Wheeler, F. J. Uribe-Salas, C. J. Conde-González, L. G. Zampilpa-Mejía, S. García-Cisneros, and M. Hernández-Avila. 2001. "Human Papillomavirus: A Highly Prevalent Sexually Transmitted Disease Agent among Female Sex Workers from Mexico City." *Sexually Transmitted Disease* 28(3): 125–130.

Juárez-Figueroa, L., F. Uribe-Salas, C. Conde-González, M. Hernández-Avila, M. Olamendi-Portugal, P. Uribe-Zúñiga, and E. Calderón. 1998. "Low Prevalence of Hepatitis B Markers among Mexican Female Sex Workers." *Sexually Transmitted Infections* 74(6): 448–450.

Kempadoo, Kamala. 1999. "Slavery or Work? Reconceptualizing Third World Prostitution." *Positions* 7(1): 225–237.

———. 2001. "Freelancers, Temporary Wives and Beach-Boys: Researching Sex Work in the Caribbean." *Feminist Review* 67: 39–62.

Kempadoo, Kamala, and Jo Doezema, eds. 1998. *Global Sex Workers: Rights, Resistance, and Redefinition.* New York: Routledge.

La Botz, Daniel. 1994. "Manufacturing Poverty: The Maquiladorization of Mexico." *International Journal of Health Services* 24(3).

Lamptey, P. 1991. "An Overview of AIDS Interventions in High-Risk Groups: Commercial Sex Workers and Their Clients." In *AIDS and Women's Reproductive Health*, edited by L. C. Chen. New York: Plenum Press.

Langley, Erika. 1997. *The Lusty Lady.* Göttingen, Germany: Scalo Books.

Leonard, L., and M. W. Ross. 1997. "The Last Sexual Encounter: The Contextualization of Sexual Risk Behavior." *International Journal of STD and AIDS* 8(10): 643–645.

Leonard, Z., and P. Thistlewaite. 1990. "Prostitution and HIV Infection." In *Women, AIDS, and Activism,* edited by C. Chris and M. Pearl. Boston: South End Press.

Lim, Lin Lean. 1998. "The Sex Sector: The Economic and Social Bases of Prostitution in Southeast Asia." International Labor Organization.

Longford, Michael. 1995. "Family Poverty and the Exploitation of Child Labor." *Law and Policy* 17(4): 471–482.

Lorey, David. 1999. *The U.S.–Mexican Border in the Twentieth Century: A History of Economic and Social Transformation.* Wilmington: SR Books.

Low, Setha. 1999. *Theorizing the City: The New Urban Anthropology Reader.* New Brunswick: Rutgers University Press.

———. 2000. *On the Plaza: The Politics of Public Space and Culture.* Austin: University of Texas Press.

Lustig, Nora. 1992. *Mexico, the Remaking of an Economy.* Washington: Brookings Institution.

Martínez, Oscar. 1996. *U.S.–Mexico Borderlands: Historical and Contemporary Perspectives.* Wilmington: SR Books.

Mathews, P. W. 1987. *Male Prostitution: Two Monographs.* Sydney: Australian Book Co.

Mbizvo, E. M., et al. 2002. "Association of Herpes Simplex Virus Type 2 with the Human Immunodeficiency Virus among Urban Women in Zimbabwe." *International Journal of STD and AIDS* 13(5): 343–348.

McCracken, Grant. 1990. *Culture and Consumption: New Approaches to the Symbolic Character of Consumer Goods and Activities.* Bloomington: Indiana University Press.

McKeganey, N., and M. Barnard. 1992. *AIDS, Drugs and Sexual Risk—Lives in the Balance.* Buckingham: Open University Press.

McLeod, E. 1982. *Working Women: Prostitutes Now.* London: Groom Helm.

Moore, J., J. S. Harrison, K. L. Kay, S. Deren, and L. S. Doll. 1995. "Factors Associated with Hispanic Women's HIV-Related Communication and Condom Use with Male Partners." *AIDS Care* 7(4): 415–427.

Morisky, D. E., T. V. Tiglao, C. D. Sneed, S. B. Tempongko, J. C. Baltazar, R. Detels, and J. A. Stein. 1998. "The Effects of Establishment Practices, Knowledge and Attitudes on Condom Use among Filipina Sex Workers." *AIDS Care* 10(2): 213–220.

Morris, M., A. Pramualratana, C. Podhisita, and M. J. Wawer. 1995. "The Relational Determinants of Condom Use with Commercial Sex Partners in Thailand." *AIDS* 9(5): 507–515.

Morse, Edward V., Patricia M. Simon, Paul M. Balson, and Howard J. Osofsky. 1992. "Sexual Behavior Patterns of Customers of Male Street Prostitutes." *Archives of Sexual Behavior* 21(4): 347–357.

MSN. 2002a. "More than Half of Mexicans Live in Poverty." Mexico Solidarity Network: Weekly News and Analysis.

———. 2002b. "New Agrarian Policies under Attack." Vol. 2002. Mexico Solidarity Network: Weekly News and Analysis.

———. 2002c. "Agriculture Threatened with Near Extinction." Mexico Solidarity Network: Weekly News and Analysis.

Nagle, Jill. 1997. *Whores and Other Feminists.* New York: Routledge.

Nelson, Lise, and Joni Seager. 2004. *A Companion to Feminist Geography*. Boston: Blackwell.

Nevins, Joseph. 2002. *Operation Gatekeeper: The Rise of the "Illegal Alien" and the Making of the U.S.–Mexico Boundary*. New York: Routledge.

Odo, C., and A. Hawelu. 2001. "Eo na Mahu o Hawai'i: The Extraordinary Health Needs of Hawai'i's Mahu." *Pacific Health Dialogue* 8(2): 327–334.

O'Dougherty, Maureen. 2002. *Consumption Intensified: The Politics of Middle-Class Daily Life in Brazil*. Durham: Duke University Press.

Outwater, A., L. Nkya, G. Lwihula, P. O'Connor, M. Leshabari, J. Nguma, B. Mwizarubi, U. Laukamm-Josten, E. C. Green, and S. E. Hassig. 2000. "Patterns of Partnership and Condom Use in Two Communities of Female Sex Workers in Tanzania." *Journal of Associated Nurses AIDS Care* 11(4): 46–54.

Parfit, Michael. 1996. "Tijuana and the Border: Magnet of Opportunity." *National Geographic* 94–107.

Parker, Richard G. 1991. *Bodies, Pleasures, and Passions: Sexual Culture in Contemporary Brazil*. Boston: Beacon Press.

———. 1999. *Beneath the Equator: Cultures of Desire, Male Homosexuality, and Emerging Gay Communities in Brazil*. New York: Routledge.

Parker, Richard G., D. Easton, and C. H. Klein. 2000. "Structural Barriers and Facilitators in HIV Prevention: A Review of International Research." *AIDS* 14 Supplement 1: S22-32.

Patton, Cindy. 1996. *Fatal Advice: How Safe-Sex Education Went Wrong*. Durham: Duke University Press.

Peña, Devon G. 1997. *The Terror of the Machine: Technology, Work, Gender and Ecology on the U.S.–Mexico Border*. Austin: University of Texas Press.

Pheterson, Gail. 1996. *The Prostitution Prism*. Amsterdam: Amsterdam University Press.

Phoenix, Joanna. 1999. *Making Sense of Prostitution*. New York: Palgrave.

Plumridge, L., and G. Abel. 2001. "A 'Segmented' Sex Industry in New Zealand: Sexual and Personal Safety of Female Sex Workers." *Australian and New Zealand Journal of Public Health* 25(1): 78–83.

Prieur, Annick. 1998. *Mema's House, Mexico City: On Transvestites, Queens, and Machos*. Chicago: University of Chicago Press.

Richards, Tom J., and Lynn Richards. 1991. "The NUDIST Qualitative Data Analysis System." *Qualitative Sociology* 14: 307–324.

Richters, J., J. Gerofi, and B. Donovan. 1995. "Why Do Condoms Break or Slip Off in Use? An Exploratory Study." *International Journal of STD and AIDS* 6(1): 11–18.

Sacks, Valerie. 1996. "Women and AIDS: An Analysis of Media Misrepresentations." *Social Science and Medicine* 42(1): 59–73.

Safa, Helen. 1995. *The Myth of the Male Breadwinner: Women and Industrialization in the Caribbean*. Boulder: Westview Press.

Sassen, Saskia. 2002. "Global Cities and Survival Circuits." In *Global Woman: Nannies, Maids, and Sex Workers in the New Economy*, edited by Barbara Ehrenreich and Arlie Russell Hochschild. New York: Metropolitan Books.

Schatz, John. 1998. Tijuana: The Dynamics of a Mexican Border City. http://www.baja-web.com/tijuana/tijuana-history2.html

SDHS, San Diego Historical Society. 2002a. Stingaree. San Diego. San Diego Historical Society Archives. Undated materials (no author).

————. 2002b. Did San Diego Have Prohibition? San Diego. San Diego Historical Society Archives. Undated materials (no author).

Singer, Merrill. 1990. "Reinventing Medical Anthropology: Toward a Critical Realignment." *Social Science and Medicine* 30(2): 179–187.

————. 1991. "Confronting the AIDS Epidemic among IV Drug Users: Does Ethnic Culture Matter?" *AIDS Education and Prevention* 3(3): 258–283.

————. 1994. "AIDS and the Health Crisis of the U.S. Urban Poor: The Perspective of Critical Medical Anthropology." *Social Science and Medicine* 39(7): 931–948.

————. 1998. "Beyond the Ivory Tower: Critical Praxis in Medical Anthropology." In *Understanding and Applying Medical Anthropology*, edited by Brown. Palo Alto: Mayfield.

————. 2001. "Toward a Bio-Cultural and Political Economic Integration of Alcohol, Tobacco and Drug Studies in the Coming Century." *Social Science and Medicine* 53(2): 199–213.

Singer, Merrill, and Hans Baer. 1995. *Critical Medical Anthropology*. Amityville, N.Y.: Baywood.

Singer, Merrill, and Arachu Castro, eds. 2004. *Unhealthy Health Policy: A Critical Anthropological Examination*. Walnut Creek, Calif.: Altamira Press.

Singer, Merrill., F. Valentin, H. Baer, and Z. Jia. 1992. "Why Does Juan Garcia Have a Drinking Problem? The Perspective of Critical Medical Anthropology." *Medical Anthropology* 14(1): 77–108.

Sobo, Elisa Janine. 1995. *Choosing Unsafe Sex: AIDS-Risk Denial among Disadvantaged Women*. Philadelphia: University of Pennsylvania Press.

Sowadsky, Rick. 1999. Lubrication (lube): What kind should I use during sex? http://www.thebody.com/Forums/AIDS/SafeSex/Archive/PreventionSexual/Q8936.html

Stevens, E. 1973. "Machismo and Marianismo." *Society* 10: 57–63.

Sycamore, Matt Bernstein. 2000. *Tricks and Treats: Sex Workers Write about Their Clients*. New York: Harrington Park Press.

Taylor, Lawrence. 2001. *Tunnel Kids*. Tucson: University of Arizona Press.

UNIFEM, United Nations Development Fund for Women. 2003. "Women, War and Peace: The Independent Experts' Assessment on the Impact of Armed Conflict on Women and Women's Role in Peace-building." In *Progress of the World's Women 2002*. Volume 1. New York: UNIFEM.

Urea, Luis Alberto. 1993. *Across the Wire: Life and Hard Times on the Mexican Border*. New York: Anchor Books, Doubleday.

Uribe-Salas, F., C. Hernández-Girón, C. Conde-González, A. Cruz-Valdez, L. Juárez-Figueroa, and M. Hernández-Avila. 1995. ["Characteristics related to STD/HIV in men working in Mexico City bars where female prostitution takes place"]. *Salud Pública Mexico* 37(5): 385–393.

Uribe-Salas, F., C. del Río Chiriboga, C. J. Conde-González, L. Juárez-Figueroa, P. Uribe-Zúñiga, E. Calderón-Jaimes, and M. Hernández-Avila. 1996. "Prevalence, Incidence, and Determinants of Syphilis in Female Commercial Sex Workers in Mexico City." *Sexually Transmitted Diseases* 23(2): 120–126.

U.S. Department of State. 2005. Trafficking in Persons Report. Released by the Office to Monitor and Combat Trafficking in Persons. http://www.state.gov/g/tip/rls/tiprpt/2005/46606.htm

Valera, R. J., R. G. Sawyer, G. R. Schiraldi. 2001. "Perceived Health Needs of Inner-City Street Prostitutes." *American Journal of Health Behavior* 25(1): 50–59.

van den Hoek, J. A., R. A. Coutinho, H. J. van Haastrecht, A. W. van Zadelhoff, and J. Goudsmit. 1988. "Prevalence and Risk Factors of HIV Injections among Drug Users and Drug Using Prostitutes in Amsterdam." *AIDS* 2(1): 55–60.

Venema, P. U., and J. Visser. 1990. "Safer Prostitution in Holland." In *AIDS, Drugs and Prostitution*, edited by M. Plant. London: Tavistock Routledge.

Wacquant, Loic. 2004. "Comment to Paul Farmer's Sidney W. Mintz Lecture for 2001: An Anthropology of Structural Violence." *Current Anthropology* 45(3): 305–325.

Waddell, Charles. 1996. "HIV and the Social World of Female Commercial Sex Workers." *Medical Anthropology Quarterly* 10(1): 75–82.

Waterman, S. H., G. Juarez, S. J. Carr, and L. Kilman. 1990. "Salmonella Arizona Infections in Latinos Associated with Rattlesnake Folk Medicine." *American Journal of Public Health* 80(3): 286–289.

Weinberg, M. S., F. M. Shaver, and C. J. Williams. 1999. "Gendered Sex Work in the San Francisco Tenderloin." *Archives of Sexual Behavior* 28(6).

Wells, Stephen Dyer. 2003. Old Tijuana Virtual Postcard Tour: Reminiscing through the Past across the Border at Tia Juana: Dig-That-Crazy-Far-Out-Planet-Man! http://www.digthatcrazyfarout.com/oldtj/

West, Donald J., with Buz de Villiers. 1993. *Male Prostitution.* New York: Haworth Press.

Wiessing, L. G., M. S. van Roosmalen, P. Koedijk, B. Bieleman, and H. Houweling. 1999. "Silicones, Hormones and HIV in Transgender Street Prostitutes." *AIDS* 13(16): 2315–2316.

Wong, M. L., R. K. Chan, D. Koh, and S. Wee. 2000. "A Prospective Study on Condom Slippage and Breakage among Female Brothel-Based Sex Workers in Singapore." *Sexually Transmitted Diseases* 27(4): 208–214.

Yin, Robert K. 1994. *Case Study Research.* 2nd edition. Thousand Oaks, Calif.: Sage Publications.

Index